The Complete
Decorative
Painter

The Complete
Decorative
Painter

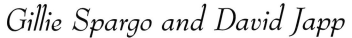

Gillie Spargo and David Japp

Colour
Library
Direct

4583

This edition published 1999 by Colour Library Direct

© 1996 Quadrillion Publishing Ltd, Godalming, Surrey

All rights reserved

Printed and bound in Italy

ISBN 1-8533-528-0

THE AUTHORS

DAVID JAPP studied art at the Dundee School of Art in Scotland, where he gained a BA with honors. He then took a Master of Arts degree at the Glasgow School of Art. Since graduating, he has worked as a decorative artist both for private and commercial clients, taking on extensive commissions throughout the world. David's skills are widely acknowledged, as is his talent for taking an unusual idea and developing it in the painted form. He is frequently called upon to run workshops in the art of decorative paint finishes worldwide.

GILLIE SPARGO originally trained as a graphic designer. Some seven years ago she began work as a diagram artist for *Woman's Weekly*, a highly popular women's interest magazine in the UK. She soon moved on to become a journalist, commissioning a wide range of homecraft projects and articles. She has recently embarked on a freelance career to produce craft projects and to undertake photographic styling for leading magazines and book projects.

THE PHOTOGRAPHERS

NELSON HARGREAVES developed his unique approach to photography through assisting the famous style magazine photographers of the 1960s. As a freelance photographer, Nelson has been in constant demand by leading magazine and book publishers for more than 20 years. He lives in rural West Sussex, England.

STEVE TANNER studied photography at the Bournemouth and Poole College of Art in the South of England. He set up his own photographic studio in 1986 and has since gained an outstanding reputation for still-life photography. His work has appeared in a wide rangeof successful homestyle books as well as leading magazines.

Credits

Managing Editor: Jo Finnis
Editor: Sue Wilkinson
Design: Phil Gorton; Stonecastle Graphics; Jill Coote
Typesetting: Elaine Morris
Production: Ruth Arthur; Sally Connolly; Neil Randles; Jonathan Tickner
Production Director: Gerald Hughes

CONTENTS

PART ONE

Paint Finishes

Introduction
pages 14-15

Materials
pages 16-17

General Preparation Notes
pages 18-19

Paints & Glazes
pages 20-21

Colour
pages 22-23

Techniques
pages 24-55

Projects
pages 56-91

Templates
page 92-97

PART TWO

Stencilling

Materials & Equipment
pages 100-101

Techniques
pages 102-111

Furniture
pages 112-127

Fabric
pages 128-141

Decorative Effects
pages 142-153

Accessories
pages 154-167

Templates
pages 168-187

PART ONE
Paint Finishes

INTRODUCTION

EXPERIMENTING WITH different paint techniques can be fun. All it takes is a little confidence and suddenly the possibilities are endless – a marbled fireplace or a slate floor all created with paint can soon become a reality. The aim of this book is to give you that confidence.

Firstly, to help achieve that confidence, the book looks at the equipment you need to get started, which includes brushes, paints and glazes. Next, you need to understand a little about the use of colour.

Each type of paint finish is looked at in-depth and every stage required to create the look is considered. This makes it as easy as possible for you to start painting the design you want.

For each type of finish, the surface preparation, suitable surfaces and the type of equipment needed are described so you know exactly what you will require. This is all backed up with step-by-step photographs which show the important stages of each technique in detail.

Once you are happy with the effects you have created, the best ways to protect the surface are considered. This means that the final finish will be as hard-wearing and durable as possible so that your work will last indefinately.

One of the most important factors to remember when using paint effects is that most mistakes can be rectified fairly easily, so never be afraid to experiment. Paint effects are also perfect for those who like to change their colour schemes or decorative styles, because you can continue to add to and adapt them. Even when a room is finished, if the effect is not quite as you intended, or if you have lived with it for a few years and want a change, then it can be easily altered by painting another glaze or tinted varnish over the original surface.

Before you start painting, you need to decide on the type of effect you want to create, the colour schemes you like, and the overall impression you want to achieve. Inspiration for this can come from absolutely anywhere. Old pattern books and reference books from the library might trigger an idea for an individual scheme; a piece of fabric or even a texture found on a piece of wood, bark or a stone.

Even small items can spark off a design – a piece of china with an unusual motif, a picture or even a bookmark. Sometimes, interior paint effects have been created from even more unusual sources, such as a favourite plant in an old terracotta pot, which can inspire interesting and successful colour combinations.

A good general rule when you are looking at your source of inspiration is to use the background colour for your largest surface area. So for walls, for example, paint or glaze them in the background colour, and then use the detail colours for the stencil or design. This principle is seen on pages 84-85, where the design for the walls has been inspired by the curtain fabric.

Remember, when taking designs from curtains for walls not to overdo the effect. Most paint finishes work best when used selectively, or when they are combined with other surface treatments, fabrics and simple flat colour bases.

Paint finishes and the use of paint techniques go back centuries, during which time they have been subject to the whims of fashion. They also offer one of the cheapest ways of transforming an ordinary room or piece of furniture into something different and special. This fact alone makes them well worth a little investigation.

Paint finishes are seen in the world's most prestigious houses, hotels and commercial properties. Why not look out for different and unusual paint techniques when you are visiting historic buildings or commercial properties?

Although it is tempting to follow each recipe or technique in the book, step-by-step, try and develop your own style and personality by experimenting. In addition, when you are trying to re-create the look of wood or marble, use a photograph or even a piece of the real thing as inspiration.

MATERIALS

LTHOUGH SPECIALIST BRUSHES are wonderful to own and use, they are not always necessary. Most of the paint effects created in this book can easily be achieved with ordinary, and even old and worn out paintbrushes, paint, glazes and other bits and pieces that you will find around the home.

A cheap dusting brush or wallpaper brush is worth buying as it can be very versatile for a whole host of finishes: dragging, stippling, flogging, distressing, graining, colour washing and even softening marbling marks.

Torn pieces of cardboard, toothbrushes, old shaving brushes, pieces of newspaper, soft rags and feathers can all be used creatively while painting, and an imaginative use of these everyday objects can quickly transform an old piece of furniture, giving it a new lease of life.

A wise investment is a natural sea sponge. Apart from making perfect marks when you are sponging, this can be used when creating a marble effect, and for softening the effect of other finishes. There is no real substitute for a natural sponge; the effect it creates would be difficult to achieve in any other way.

Another good buy is a 'rocker' or heartgrainer, which is used when creating a painted wood effect. You can use the rocker to make the open heartgrain effect which you find in oak or pine. These marks would take ages to create with other tools as the heartgrainer simply creates a series of close, fine lines. The heartgrainer is also useful when you want to achieve a moiré effect, which again would be very difficult to produce with any of the other tools.

A fairly low-tack masking tape is another must when creating some painted finishes. Not only is it useful for the simple task of masking off areas which do not need painting, it is also useful for marking up areas which should have straight lines,

and for sticking down pieces of fabric or swatches next to the paint area when you are checking your mixed paint colours. You can see a good example of how useful masking tape can be on page 58-63 where it has been used to create a realistic trellis effect in a mural.

When painting, you will also need somewhere to mix colours. Any tray with a lip will do the job, but you'll find that the best item for this is a paint roller tray, which is fairly inexpensive.

A supply of small glass jars is useful to hold water, turpentine or even a range of mixed up coloured glazes. Small glass jars are also handy for holding small quantities of water-based paint while you are working, rather than trying to deal with larger cans.

Old sheets torn into small rags or newspaper will be needed when you are ragging or dragging. Newspaper is also essential for covering up areas such as carpets and floors to avoid splashes and spills. If you do need an instant clean-up, liquid detergent is worth having on hand. It can also be added to water-based glazes, to make them more useable.

Another essential is a roll or pack of tissue paper. This is not only used when ragging, it is also perfect for softening some effects, and for instant clean-ups on the painted surfaces. Tissue will quickly and easily remove any paint runs or smudges which often occur by mistake. Tissue is also handy for drying brushes.

For drawing straight lines you will need a ruler or an old piece of dado rail. String is essential if you want to draw circles and is also needed for making makeshift plumb lines with a weight. To draw a circle, simply tie a pencil to a length of string, then hold the string down where you want the centre of the circle to be. Now, using the taut piece of string as the radius draw the circle. For the inner circle shorten, the length of string.

GENERAL PREPARATION NOTES

These GENERAL NOTES on preparation apply to all surfaces unless a specific surface is required. For oil-based finishes, which are the majority of the finishes found in this book, whether on walls, furniture or objects, the base to which you apply the glaze has to be completely non-absorbent.

To achieve this, you first need to create a smooth flat surface. Fill any surface holes or dents, then carefully rub down, sand with fine grade sandpaper and wipe off any excess dust. Then, if necessary, repeat this process until all the dents are smoothed over before painting. Clean and wipe down, then vacuum the area to eliminate as much dust as possible.

Very porous surfaces, such as lined or plaster walls, must then be sealed with either PVA medium (polyvinyl acetate medium), unibond or emulsion thinned half and half with water. If you are working on new wood, give it a coat of proprietary oil or acrylic-based primer. Leave to dry completely.

Metal objects should be smoothed off with a wire brush or emery paper and then cleaned with turpentine and rags. They will need a coat of metal primer at this stage.

Once the surface has been smoothed down and cleaned off, apply a coat of oil-based undercoat or eggshell – never gloss – thinned slightly with turpentine. Leave this to dry overnight.

When the surface is dry, smooth down again with a piece of fine-grade 'flour' paper. This will remove all the small hairs and pieces of grit which may have settled on the surface while it dried.

Finally, apply another coat of undercoat or eggshell, and again leave the surface to dry.

If you are working with a previously painted or varnished object which is in a reasonable condition it can simply be 'keyed' by sanding with a medium or fine sandpaper, which basically provides a bind for the new paint to adhere to.

If working on a previously waxed surface, the wax needs to be removed before the painting can start. Do this by rubbing the surface with steel wool and tupentine, repeating the process until all the wax is removed. Then, lightly sand the surface with sandpaper.

As with everything, there are some exceptions to these rules. Sponging can be done on almost any surface straight away, providing that the surface is stable, ie, no peeling paper or cracking plaster. It is even one of the few finishes which can be applied to woodchip.

When a colour wash is applied to a flat emulsion as opposed to a silky or slightly shiny emulsion, it will sink in like blotting paper, and look patchy. However, if you build up the surface, layer by layer, you can achieve a very pleasing overall effect.

Another good idea at preparation stage is to prepare two or three boards or cards in the same way as the wall or object. These can then be used to try out the paints, glazes and colours and generally practice on before working on the object itself. Making these boards will not take long to do, but will help with building up confidence, and will also be useful at various stages of the finish.

Lastly, you will find that some finishes need more preparation than others, but you should not be put off attempting them because of this. A little practice at the early stages will pay off in the long run, especially if you want the finish to be durable.

PAINTS AND GLAZES

ONCE YOU HAVE DECIDED on the finish you want, you need to decide on the medium you are going to work in: water or oil.

Several finishes, including many of the popular ones such as sponging, colour washing, graining and distressing, can be created in either medium, so it is up to the individual which one is used.

Most finishes, however, are executed in oils. As a medium, oil is much easier to manipulate, which makes it more suitable for paint finishes. Oils also have a longer drying time and are generally more hard-wearing once dry than water-based paints. They are ideal for furniture, fitted bedrooms, kitchens and bathrooms.

Water-based finishes are by contrast generally less hard-wearing, unless they are well-varnished. They also tend to dry quickly, so are not particularly easy to handle or manipulate. There is one advantage to this, however, if you want to build up layers quickly, especially when sponging or colour washing. The speed of drying means an average sized room can be finished in a day even if you decide to build up four or five different layers of colour.

Other finishes like verdigris use a mixed medium. Many finishes also include the use of cellulose-based sprays.

Whatever medium you choose, you will soon discover that a glaze is much more versatile than paint, in that once it has been applied to a surface it can be manipulated easily and the marks and effects can be more easily achieved. Glazes can also be built up in layers, achieving a depth and movement which cannot be maintained by using proprietary paints straight from a can.

Proprietary scumble glaze is the main ingredient of most glazes, and can be bought from good decorating stores. This almost transparent medium extends the drying times and also retains the marks that you make. It is essential when working on a large area using a glaze to keep a wet edge going so you avoid having any bad breaks which will show as lines, patches or dry areas.

It is not a good idea to use a scumble glaze straight from the can, since it would take too long to dry. A good formula for a glaze would be a mixture of 50 per cent scumble and 50 per cent turpentine. The colour is then added either from a tube of artists' oil paint or from an oil-based eggshell. As a rule when mixing a glaze the more scumble glaze you add the longer you will have to manipulate it, and the longer it takes to dry. The more turpentine you add, the thinner the glaze.

When it comes to colour itself, eggshell paint gives you a thicker mix, whereas adding artists' oils gives the advantage of pure colour without losing the clear consistency of the glaze.

It is best to start experimenting with a 50:50 ratio of scumble glaze to turpentine, and play with this glaze to find out what works for you. The results will vary depending on the item you are decorating, so make up each glaze as you need it. The type of colour you add also depends on preference, and on the object you are painting. Add a little colour at a time, testing it on a board until you are satisfied. If you decide to use artists' oils, mix the colour into a small amount of glaze or turpentine first before adding it to the main glaze. This will avoid the problem of lumps of pure colour. Remember, too, that oil-based glazes may darken in areas deprived of light.

When using water-based finishes, it is easier to buy your colour in a proprietary emulsion and thin it with water or a water-based emulsion glaze. If you need to alter the colour, use acrylics, or their equivalent, which can be bought from art suppliers. Again, mix these colours in a little glaze before adding to the main glaze.

Be particularly careful when handling toxic or hazardous materials. Always follow the manufacturer's instructions and ensure that the area you are working in is well-ventilated. Use plastic gloves and masks when possible.

Always lay rags charged with scumble glaze out flat to dry before disposing of them since they are liable to combust when wet.

COLOUR

COLOUR IS PROBABLY the most predominant feature of any paint effect, and yet colour mixing is a difficult thing to try to teach. It is really something only learnt by trial, error and patience, although there are some basic principles which can act as a sound starting point.

When you are mixing colours, it is important to remember that colour is a personal thing. Different people react to colours in a variety of ways, and you must bear this in mind so that you consciously choose colours which create the right atmosphere for you. Consider colours in relation to their surroundings and never in isolation.

When decorating a room, think of the overall atmosphere you want to achieve. Do you want to create a light room or a warm and intimate room? Is it a cold room needing to be made cosier? Do you want to make a small room appear larger, or a large room less daunting? Do you want to lower a ceiling or make a feature of an alcove? The colours you choose and their tonal values will go a long way to addressing some of these problems.

Remember, too, that colours change dramatically in different lights: daylight, electric light, spotlights or subtle downlighters. So you will need to think about the style of your lighting in the overall plan. Finally, though, it is about personal instincts and personal preferences, and a little common sense is useful at this stage.

The principles of colour can get a little complicated, but again if you apply that same common sense you can avoid problems. There is no need to get bogged down or frightened off by so called 'rules' about primary, complementary, tertiary or discordant colours. If you are interested in finding out about the principles, fine, but don't let the rules scare you or make the subject seem too complicated.

When you start to think about colours, remember the designs and patterns that inspire you and try to use those colours. It will give you more confidence when you think that these colours were originally created by a designer. Use the background colour on the design for your largest painted area, then introduce lighter and darker tones of the same colour, or pick other colours from the object to create interest, depth and more detail.

If you mix your own colours and glazes rather than using proprietary mixes, you will need a basic palette of colours either in artists' oil colours, oil-based glazes and finishes, or good quality acrylics for finishing water-based glazes.

A basic palette of red, blue and yellow, (cadmium red, French ultramarine and cadmium yellow, for example) would provide your three primary and main sources of colour. Assuming you do not want to use the colours pure, you need to transform them into viable decorating colours. A good range of earth colours would be burnt umber, burnt sienna, raw umber, raw sienna and yellow ochre. Black can be useful, and you'll need white. The earth colours are excellent for improving the quality of colour, and will work better than black if you want to darken or add depth to a colour. Black makes colours look duller.

Once you have pulled together your basic palette, you will be able to mix most of the colours you will need.

Some finishes require particular colours. Lapis lazuli, for example, will need Prussian blue, which cannot be made from this basic palette. Deep red or a particular green are difficult to mix, so in these cases buy the actual colour.

Another alternative is to use universal stainers with a colour. The main advantage with these is that they mix both with water- and oil-based materials, but they do not give such a feeling of quality as the artists' oils. When using proprietary materials, it is important to follow the manufacturer's instructions since these may vary between brands.

Gain confidence by experimenting with colours first. Squeeze a little of each colour on to a white board, then add a tiny amount of one of the "earth" colours, or a little white.

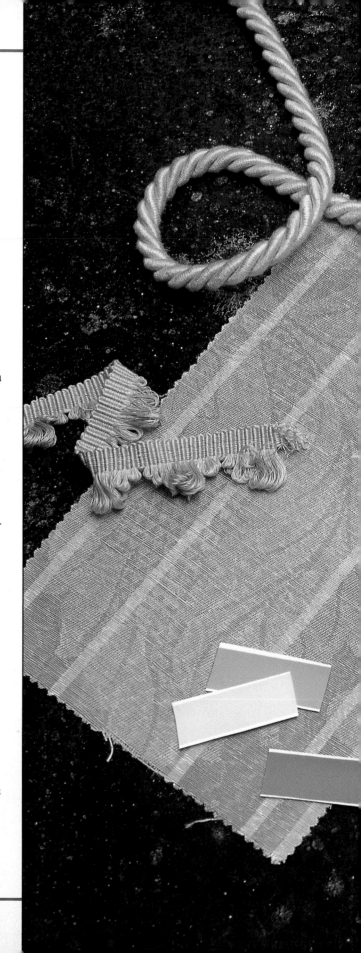

TECHNIQUES

$\mathcal{A}$lmost every paint technique
you are ever likely to want to create is included here,
from realistic lapis lazuli and malachite, to the more simple
but very effective sponging and ragging effects.
Every stage of each process is clearly explained and illustrated with
the aid of step-by-step photographs.
Wherever necessary, diagrams have been included
to make the specific techniques even more accessible.
Once you are happy with your final effect,
the best way to protect your surface is also considered.

RAGGING AND STIPPLING

THESE FINISHES are similar in technique, in that a glaze is applied and then manipulated with either a brush, rag or newspaper.

Both finishes should be applied to a well-prepared surface. A surface painted with two coats of eggshell is ideal. You could use a water-based glaze, but for a more professional finish try an oil-based mixture of at least 50 per cent scumble.

Stippling is a sophisticated finish and is best done in one layer, while ragging can be built up in layers. Working with layers, leave the first layer to dry completely before applying the next. Experiment with rags, newspapers and polythene before you decide on your finished effect.

Proper stippling brushes are ideal for stippling but are expensive. A large light wallpaper or dusting brush achieves a similar effect. Rotate your hand, when off the surface, to avoid creating a pattern.

1 Apply the glaze evenly using a soft brush. Work the glaze drawing a basket weave effect using light brush strokes to achieve an even coverage.

2 Crumple a rag or cloth so that it is easy to grip. Dab the glaze with the rag, turning your hand as you work. This will avoid a regular pattern being created.

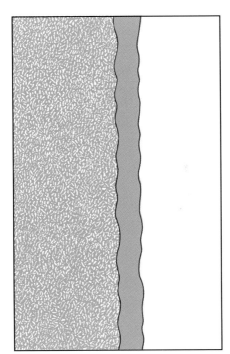

ABOVE: Working a wet edge is important for both finishes. On large areas, one person could apply the glaze while the other rags.

3 To create a softer look, rag off more of the glaze with a soft dry rag using the same technique as before. Stand back occasionally to check you are happy with the effect. Change the rag as necessary.

LEFT: A mid-tone red, oil-based eggshell
has been ragged with a deep crimson glaze
to give a very dramatic effect, which is
enhanced by subtle lighting.

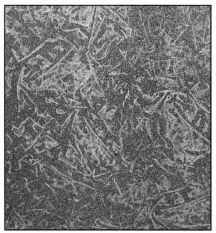

4 This is another way of creating a
ragged effect. The wall has been
stippled beforehand to eliminate any brush
marks, which show with ordinary ragging.

5 A ragged background is ideal for a
stencilled frieze or border. In this case,
a stippled gold stencil is painted on a deep
red, ragged background.

1 When stippling, apply the glaze evenly,
then use a dry, stippling brush or
wallpaper brush to stipple the area. If you
are putting glaze back on to the surface, the
brush is too wet.

2 Stippling is a delicate effect which
lends itself to strong colours. Tint the
glaze with artists' oils rather than eggshell,
which thickens the glaze, and give the glaze
more movement by using 60 per cent
scumble to 40 per cent turpentine.

DRAGGING

THIS PAINT EFFECT is a straightforward and simplified version of woodgraining, which can be achieved on most reasonably smooth, oil-based surfaces. The effect can be created using a variety of different glazes. Although the technique works on walls, it is best on woodwork. You can use any brush, but old brushes sometimes give a more attractive effect. On walls, always drag the brush from the top to about halfway down, then drag up, easing the pressure and lifting the brush off the wall as it passes the area already dragged. Vary the height of this break.

Keep the brush as dry as possible as it quickly absorbs glaze. If a flogging effect (a looser combed look) is required, hit the panel at random as you work down. Use a standard oil-based mixture of 50 per cent scumble to 50 per cent turpentine.

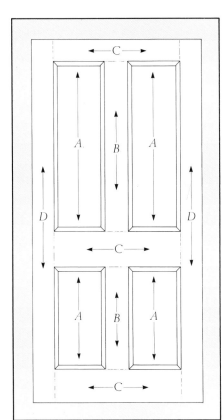

1 Apply the glaze evenly on one panel. Take a firm brush and drag down from the top of the panel to the bottom. Then, lightly drag up to lift the build of glaze.

2 Once the panels and mouldings have been dragged, drag the middle verticals, the horizontals and finally the two side verticals to echo the grain of the door.

LEFT: *Drag the middle panels A first, then drag the two vertical panels B, then the three horizontal panels C. Finish by dragging the vertical side panels D.*

3 From this detailed shot of a dragged door, you can see how the brush directions work.

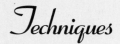

ABOVE: *This close-up detail of the living room in the main picture shows how subtle and stylish a dragged effect can be.*

ABOVE: *The dragging technique has been worked around the panels of this wardrobe, while the main panels have been ragged. The two techniques work well here.*

LEFT: *Although subtle, the walls in this living room have been dragged using a sunshine yellow glaze. Teamed with dark woods and soft, inviting sofas, the room looks very relaxing.*

SPONGING

SPONGING IS PROBABLY the quickest, easiest and most versatile of all the paint finishes. The finish can be worked on almost any surface, even woodchip, and any mistakes can be rectified fairly easily.

You need a sponge that is large enough to sit comfortably in your hand. It is best to buy a natural sponge for this technique, although you could modify a decorating sponge by tearing pieces from it so that it makes good marks.

If you are sponging walls, use a water-based emulsion and thin it slightly with water. If you are working on wood, use a slightly thinned, oil-based eggshell which will be more durable. You can also use this paint technique on smaller objects.

Pour some of your paint into a tray, then dip the damp sponge into the paint. Dab off any excess paint before working.

1 Dab the sponge on to the wall, working with a constant pressure but varying the angle to avoid making clear patterns. Work as close to the corners as possible.

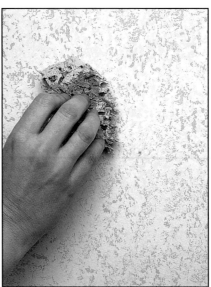

2 Leave the first colour to dry. Ensure the sponge is clean, then apply a second coat, either a second colour or another shade of the same colour.

3 Once the second coat has dried, you could add a further colour, or a lighter shade of the original. Remember that the final colour will be dominant.

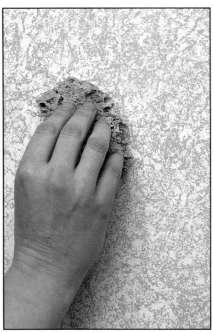

4 Finally, the last colour or shade can be sponged over the surface. Again, this should not be added until all the other colours have dried.

5 For corners and skirtings, use a small artists' brush, or a fitch, to fill in the colours. Do this while you are working each colour rather than at the end.

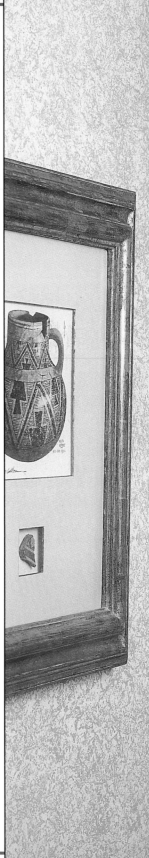

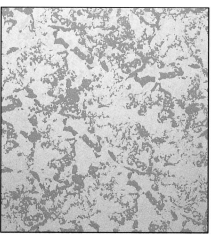

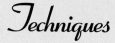

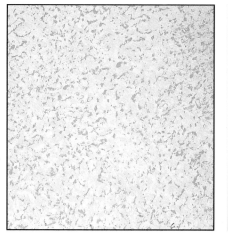

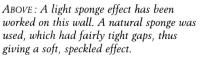

ABOVE: *A light sponge effect has been worked on this wall. A natural sponge was used, which had fairly tight gaps, thus giving a soft, speckled effect.*

ABOVE: *This is a more dramatic sponge effect, created by pushing the sponge down harder on to the wall and using a sponge with much larger holes.*

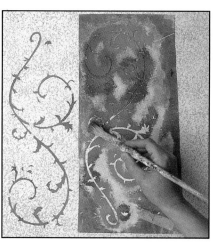

ABOVE: *A quick and easy way to tone down a colour is to work a layer of white all over the effect.*

ABOVE: *A sponged background is great for stencilling on. Here, an interesting frieze is created with a blue and red stencilled design.*

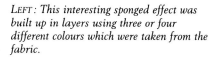

LEFT: *This interesting sponged effect was built up in layers using three or four different colours which were taken from the fabric.*

COLOUR WASHING

THIS TECHNIQUE lends itself to a rustic country look, but it is versatile enough to be used in most settings if suitable colours are used. The effect works best when using earthy colours such as Venetian red or raw sienna.

For this technique to be effective, the paint should be built up in layers. This helps to create a look with more depth.

This paint effect can be created using either an oil- or a water-based paint, but it is quicker and easier to work with water-based paints. Mix a small amount of your chosen colours in the paint and then thin the mix down with water to a ratio of 50:50. If this is still too thick, simply add more water. Although this technique can be worked on a smooth wall, we have created a slightly rough background surface to enhance the finish.

1 To prepare a surface, spread a thin layer of fine plaster over the wall. When dry, seal with emulsion thinned with water, then paint with two coats of emulsion paint.

2 When the base coat has dried, use a large brush to paint the prepared mixture on to the surface. Work quickly and evenly.

3 For a more distressed look, rub the glaze into the surface with a dry brush. Clean it on a rag as you work. Repeat if the effect is patchy.

4 To achieve a dusty, aged look to the colour washed effect, paint another layer of off-white, water-based paint thinned with water over the surface.

5 Before the off-white paint has dried, rub the paint into the surface using a dry brush. Again, dry the brush on a rag as you work.

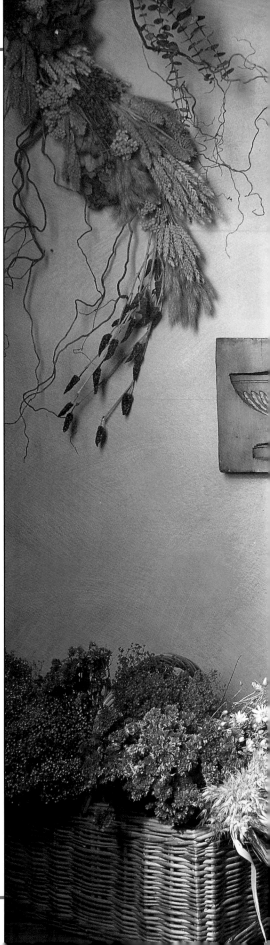

ABOVE: *The walls above the dado rail have been treated with a yellow colour wash. The dado has a crackled paint effect, and the cabinet has been stencilled, then aged.*

ABOVE: *Although often considered as a rustic wall treatment, colour washing can work well anywhere in the home. Here, it is found in a modern living room, giving extra depth to plain walls.*

ABOVE: *A simple colour wash can be quickly transformed with the addition of other colours. Here, a proprietary stencil was used to enhance the final effect.*

LEFT: *Colour washing is perfect for creating a rustic look. The technique used in this kitchen creates a homely, country look.*

ABOVE: *Looking at the stencil more clearly, you can see how paint effects such as colour washing and stencilling work so well together if the colour themes are matched considerately.*

33

SPATTERING

SPATTERING IS A VERY simple, straightforward paint technique to achieve, but it is also much more than a light-hearted effect. If used thoughtfully, for example spattering with a variety of grey, black and white paints, it can add depth to a painted object. And by simply spattering a little brown over the surface, the overall effect could even be made to look like granite.

Although this effect can be created on walls, it is very messy to execute so it is better worked on smaller objects like letter racks or lampshades.

Try experimenting with different colour combinations on a piece of card, before you work on the final item. Remember that the size of the spattering dots depends on how close the brush is to the object and how much paint there is on the brush.

1 Dip your brush in the first colour, in this case black, then hit it against a piece of wood aiming at the area you want to spatter.

2 Wash the brush after the first coat, then repeat the process with the second colour, in this case grey.

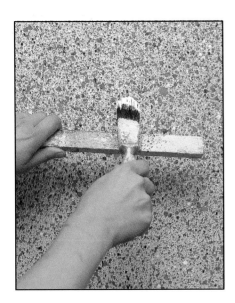

3 Repeat the process again using a third colour, in this case white. When spattering, there is no need to wait for one colour to dry before proceeding to the next.

4 This is the same process, using black, grey and white paint, but worked over a dark grey, rather than a white background.

5 Spattering can create a range of different effects. The door on the left has been given a metallic paint finish, enhanced using the spattering technique.

RIGHT: *Some of the selection of spattered objects here have been enhanced with gold and black stencils or borders.*

LIMING

Historically, wood was limed to protect it, but the technique has grown in popularity as a way of simply enhancing the characteristics of wood. The technique is particularly good for open grain woods such as oak, and also works well on moulded or carved surfaces, where it helps to highlight the carpenter's craft. Providing the object to be limed is stable and solid in structure, the technique should work well. First, clean the object thoroughly and remove any wax or previous varnishes. The best way to achieve this is to use steel wool and turpentine.

There are a number of different materials you can use to achieve a limed effect. White emulsion thinned with water, thinned oil-based white undercoat or thinned eggshell are all good. Alternatively, you could use a proprietary liming wax. Here, we have used 70 per cent oil-based undercoat thinned with turpentine.

1 Use a wire brush to lift the grain. Always brush in the direction of the grain and never across the grain.

2 Apply the liming mixture with a paintbrush, working one panel at a time. Work the mixture into the grain and in to any mouldings or cavities.

ABOVE: The main door has been treated with a simple white liming mixture, while the small door has been painted with a coloured liming mixture. Any colour of paint could be used to achieve this effect.

3 Leave the mixture on the object for a few minutes, then wipe off excess paint with a hard cloth – hessian is ideal. Repeat the process if you wipe off too much.

4 This is an example of liming an object in a different colour. A small quantity of green paint was added to the liming mixture to achieve this effect.

TORTOISESHELLING

THE INSPIRATION behind the paint technique of tortoiseshelling comes from the Far East. In these countries they used the shell of the sea tortoise as an inlay for small pieces of furniture. As traders travelled, these items were introduced to the West. However, by the nineteenth century the turtle was declared an endangered species, and the paint technique became popular.

This technique is particularly successful when it is used on small objects. While painting, bear in mind that real tortoiseshell comes in an infinite variety of marks. Almost any combination of raw sienna, burnt sienna, burnt umber, crimson and black can be used. It is best to experiment with different proportions of colour. For example, paint a large area of raw sienna, with small areas of burnt umber and black.

Badger hair brushes were used to soften this effect, but they are expensive and environmentally unfriendly. An alternative is a soft dusting brush, worked delicately.

Before you start, ensure that the working surface is as smooth as possible. Prepare the surface with a coat of golden, yellow oil-based eggshell. Protect the finished effect with at least two coats of high gloss oil-based varnish.

1 Paint a clear glaze (50:50 scumble to turpentine) over the surface. Then, using a small brush and an artists' oil-based raw sienna, paint diagonal marks.

2 Using the same brush, repeat the process with burnt sienna and covering more of the working area.

3 Again, repeat the process using burnt umber and filling in even more of the working area.

5 As an option, dab a piece of crumpled newspaper over the surface, or use a natural sea sponge dipped in turpentine.

4 Using a soft dusting or pasting brush, gently blend the colours together. Take care not to blend too much or you will loose the contrasts.

6 Soften the newspaper effect by again brushing the soft dusting brush or pasting brush over the surface.

7 Finish off by dipping the tip of a toothbrush into black oil paint mixed with a little turpentine, and lightly spatter the surface to add interest and depth.

8 *Enhance the final effect by painting in small areas of black using a small brush. Work carefully and use a small amount of paint.*

ABOVE: The top photograph shows the first stages when creating the tortoiseshell paint effect on this frame (seen left) using different proportions of colour. And, just above, you can see the finishing touches being picked out with gold paint.

LEFT: The tortoiseshell paint effect works best on smaller items. Here, it has been used on the candle holder and around a bathroom mirror. It works so effectively it could almost be the real thing. This effect always looks sumptuous and expensive.

MALACHITE AND LAPIS LAZULI

MALACHITE IS A semi-precious mineral which is sometimes used as a source for green pigments, but is often found in its polished state in jewellery. As a finish, therefore, it is most effective if used selectively.

Before you begin, try to obtain either a piece of malachite or a picture of malachite to work from. Try not to copy this, but aim for a similar design. The basic look is a dark green, highly-polished effect which is often highlighted with gold details.

This paint technique is worked on a mid-emerald green base, which should be painted with an oil-based paint. You will need a 50 per cent scumble to 50 per cent turpentine glaze, and artists' oil colours in viridian, raw umber and Prussian blue.

Lapis lazuli was also used as a source for ultramarine pigment, but because of this use it became quite scarce, and hence became popular in its polished form as a gemstone. Like malachite, the paint technique is best used on small items.

The paint finish should create a milky effect with gold and white flecks floating in a deep ultramarine glaze. Both of these techniques are applied to a smooth surface. Protect the effect with two coats of high gloss oil-based varnish.

1 Viridian is the predominant colour in malachite. Paint the three colours on to the work surface, stippling and blending to create a predominately green layer.

2 Lightly score different sized pieces of card and tear along the score lines. Use these edges to make broken circles in the stipple glaze, varying the size of marks.

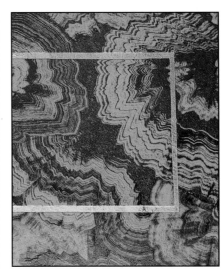

4 The malachite paint effect can easily be enhanced with gold paint. Mask off the area before painting.

3 Once you are completely happy with the result, leave the paint to dry completely. Then, protect the surface with a couple of coats of gloss varnish.

5 Here is the finished box complete with gold details.

RIGHT: *Set against a lapis lazuli table, the two green boxes have been treated with a malachite paint finish then finished with gold stencilling on the lids.*

1 Paint a clear glaze on to a white oil basecoat. Stipple artists' oil colours, over this. French ultramarine predominates but Prussian blue and raw umber are used.

2 As an option, add interest by crumpling a rag or newspaper and using this to dab the surface lightly in places.

3 Carefully soften the effect using a soft dusting brush.

4 Mix a little gold paint with white spirit and use a toothbrush to flick this paint on to the surface. Repeat with white paint.

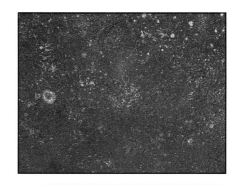

RIGHT: A detail of the finished lapis lazuli table shows the depth and purity of colour which can be achieved.

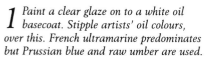

AGEING AND DISTRESSING

THERE ARE A NUMBER of ways to make an object look older than it really is. The most dramatic of these is to throw stones and buckshot at the object, but this may not really have the desired effect. A less drastic method is to start by rubbing off all the hard, sharp edges and corners, then paint the object with a dark background colour; a deep red or dark brown is perfect. Then apply a thick coat of wallpaper paste to the object. For more dramatic cracks, add a little gum arabic to the paste. Leave the coating to dry completely.

Once the object has dried, coat the whole area with a heavy coat of off-white matt emulsion, then dry it with a hairdryer on the hottest setting. If after ten minutes no cracks appear, mix a little more gum arabic into the wallpaper paste and repeat the process.

1 Sand the surface. Apply a water-based colour over the whole area. Leave to dry. Then apply a thick coat of wallpaper paste and gum arabic. Leave to dry.

2 Apply a coat of off-white matt emulsion or an alternative water-based paint over the top of the paste.

3 Once this coat of paint has been applied, dry the whole area with a hairdryer on maximum heat. Cracks should appear fairly quickly.

4 Mix a small quantity of raw sienna and raw umber acrylic paint with a little water and paint over the surface, rubbing it into the cracks.

5 Using a dry brush, rub in more ageing colour, and if necessary rub other areas smooth with sandpaper to reveal the darker colour underneath.

6 To take this ageing a stage further, mix a little raw umber acrylic with water and spatter this at random with a toothbrush.

7 Add some finishing touches by picking out areas with a further colour. Here, we have used a gold wax pigment.

LEFT: *The subtle use of the distressing technique on this bathroom sink unit shows how effective the finished results can be.*

8 Rub the wax pigment on and in with a rag, or mix the wax with a little white spirit and paint the mixture on.

CRACKLE GLAZING

GIVE A FAVOURITE POSTER or picture an authentic antiqued look using the crackle glaze technique. Although there are a number of ways to achieve this 'craquelure' effect, it is easiest to use a proprietary cracking varnish, available from most artists' suppliers.

Basically the size of the cracks depends on the time you wait between steps 1 and 2. The longer the time gap, the smaller the cracks will be.

If you use a proprietary cracking medium, you may not need to use a hairdryer since the cracks should appear within an hour.

At this stage, you have to look carefully for cracks. These will be enhanced by the ageing colour. Once you are happy with the cracked effect, squeeze some raw umber on to a piece of card or tray and mix with a tiny amount of turpentine until you have a smooth paste. (As an alternative you can experiment with other colours like terre verte.) Apply the paste over the whole area, rubbing it gently into the cracks with soft cotton wool. Then clean the excess off with a clean piece of cotton wool. Leave the surface to dry completely and protect the area with a coat of oil-based varnish.

1 Seal the picture with a colourless oil-based varnish and leave it to dry overnight. Once dry, apply a second coat of oil-based varnish thinly and evenly.

2 When the second coat is tacky but not sticky ($^1/_2$–3 hours) apply a thin, even coat of water-based cracking varnish with a clean, dry, soft brush.

3 If no cracks appear after about 30 minutes, gently heat the surface with a hairdryer. As soon as some cracks do appear, stop heating.

4 After the cracks have appeared, leave the picture to dry for a few hours, then mix a little turpentine with a little burnt umber in artists' oil.

5 Take a lump of cotton wool and gently rub this mixture into the cracks.

6 Remove the excess mixture with clean cotton wool.

7 To enhance the aged look, use a toothbrush to spatter the surface with a mixture of turpentine and raw umber.

1 For an alternative look, work a light mix of raw umber into the cracks.

2 The crackle glaze effect also works well when highlighted with another paint colour. Gold is used here, but a deep red is also very effective.

RIGHT: *The same effect has been applied to a piece of furniture which has been made from MDF (medium density fibreboard), but the technique has worked so well it could almost be an antique.*

LEFT: *The poster here has been treated with crackle glaze, while the frame has been treated with the alternative cracking method on page 40.*

MARBLING

THIS IS A CLASSICAL TECHNIQUE which should be used selectively to be convincing. It is best done on areas which might have been made from the real thing, such as fireplaces or architectural details. For inspiration, it helps to have a piece of real marble or a photograph at hand. Rather than recreating the piece accurately, be inspired by the general feeling of the marks and colours. Most importantly, don't overdo it when you are marbling. If you reach a stage that is satisfactory, leave the area to dry overnight and if necessary work on the effect the next day. Any mistakes can then be wiped off. Good preparation and a smooth surface is essential. It is best to work on a smooth, oil-based surface.

This section shows a variety of ways to achieve a marbled effect. You can use a combination of these marks. An ideal glaze is 50 per cent scumble or oil-based varnish with 50 per cent turpentine, then add the artists' oil colours of your choice.

Most people find veining the hardest to do. It is important to avoid wormy-looking veins; they should be aggressive-looking. A way of making the veins look less contrived is to use the hand you do not normally work with. Protect the finished effect with two coats of oil-based varnish.

1 Working on a white basecoat, mix a little raw sienna with the glaze and apply it in patches, moving diagonally across the surface.

2 Mix a little grey with more of the glaze and fill in the remaining areas, feathering the two colours together to blend in places.

3 Take a rag or newspaper, depending on the effect required, and dab the painted area lightly in places.

4 Dip the tip of a damp natural sea sponge into turpentine and dab some areas of the surface. This causes the glaze to spread, so be careful not to overdo this.

5 Using a soft dusting brush, very gently soften and blend the effect.

6 Pull a feather dipped in turpentine across the glaze in diagonal movements. This is called negative veining.

7 Soften some areas of this veining. The sharper marks you don't soften will look as if they are on the surface.

8 *Dip your feather in a coloured glaze or an artists' oil colour and work another series of veins flowing in a different direction. This is called positive veining.*

9 *Again, soften some areas of this veining to give the feeling of depth.*

10 *Spatter some turpentine or colour on to the area to disperse more glaze or to apply more colour.*

11 *If necessary, you can dip the sea sponge into a coloured glaze and sponge on more colour.*

LEFT : *Here, an inexpensive wooden fire surround has been painted with a marble paint effect, and looks incredibly realistic.*

LEFT : *The marbling paint effect usually works best on areas which may have been made from marble. The lampbase here is perfect for this treatment.*

MARBLING
PANELS

ONE OF THE MOST important things about achieving a solid marble feel is the final varnish. At least two coats of gloss or satin varnish will enhance the look. But if you want to take the effect further by creating a panelled look, use a tinted glaze and work this over the marbled paint effect before varnishing.

Firstly, choose the panelling you want, making sure that the size is relevant to the object itself.

If you are still finding it difficult to decide on the type of marbling you want, it may be best to consult architectural or art history books in the library.

Generally, a panel is created over a marble paint effect. Once you have marbled the area, leave it to dry, then experiment with different marks, a variety of tinted varnishes and unusual washes.

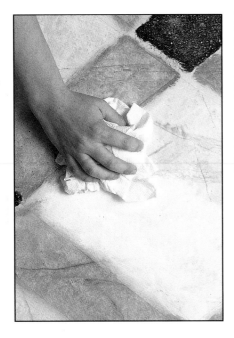

1 Mask off the panel shapes. Then mix an oil-based varnish with turpentine and tint. Apply this to some panels using a rag, allowing the underlying marbling to show.

2 Repeat the process on the second, larger panel but use a different coloured varnish. Here, grey is used.

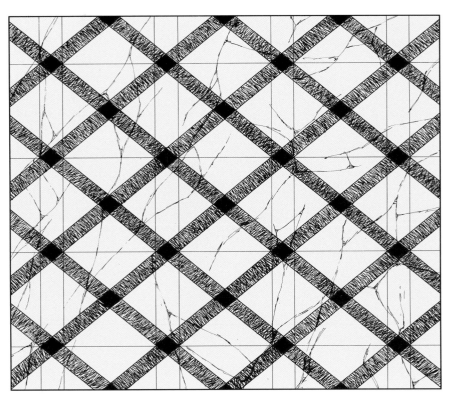

3 The smaller diamonds can then be picked out in another colour (black).

LEFT: As an alternative, this style of panelling is particularly suited to a floor.

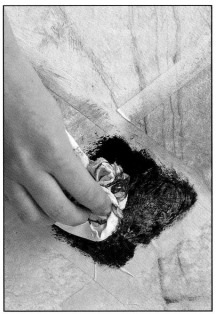

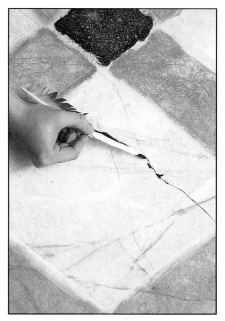

4 *When using black, rag off some of the colour with a soft cloth to take the colour's harshness away.*

5 *While the black is still wet, add another effect by dipping a toothbrush in white oil paint thinned with turpentine and spatter this over the black area.*

6 *Another natural effect you may wish to try is to add some more veins with the feather, or even to highlight the ones which are underneath.*

7 *When the glazes have dried a little but are not completely dry, carefully peel away the masking tape and wipe off any excess glaze with a rag.*

LEFT: *This is one of many different panel designs which could be used when creating a marbled panel effect.*

8 *Before varnishing, use a hard pencil to define the lines and shapes more clearly, if you want.*

ABOVE: *The paint effect panels here would work well if used for a flooring, especially in a kitchen or bathroom.*

VERDIGRIS

THIS IS THE NATURAL result of condensation on copper, bronze and brass, which in the past has been used for making green pigments. The green-blue deposit, although toxic, has a wonderfully pure look about it and, coupled with the ageing air it achieves, it is an important effect to try and imitate. It is also a super technique to experiment with and will work on a variety of surfaces. This is a good technique to use on small, decorative items as well as larger architectural features, such as the staircase seen in the main picture.

Mix the colours you need using acrylics or buy water-based emulsions and tint them with acrylics to obtain the colours. Protect the finish with oil-based varnish.

1 Spray or paint the object with a base colour of copper, gold or bronze. Then, leave to dry. Now, using a small brush, stipple the darker colour all over the object.

2 Using a rag, dab and stipple the paint, lifting it off in some areas and leaving it on in others, particularly in recesses. Leave to dry.

3 Using a small brush, add the second lighter colour on top of the first, again working a random effect.

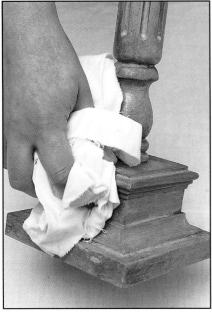

4 Using a rag, dab some of the second colour off, exposing the first and bronze colours underneath. Leave to dry.

5 Using a small brush, paint an off-white, water-based paint thinned with 20 per cent water over the area.

6 *Immediately this is on, rag it off again leaving only traces of the white paint, particularly in the recessed areas, to give the object a dusty look. Leave to dry.*

7 *Rub the raised areas gently with a fine sandpaper or a kitchen scourer to expose more of the colours underneath.*

8 *As a final touch, spatter a little raw umber on to the finished surface with a toothbrush.*

ABOVE : *The final lampbase looks very effective once the verdigris treatment has been completed.*

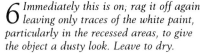

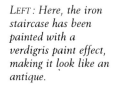

LEFT: *Here, the iron staircase has been painted with a verdigris paint effect, making it look like an antique.*

ABOVE : *The paint colours which were used.*

TERRACOTTA

THIS WEATHERED TERRACOTTA look is easy to create and can even be painted on to walls if used sensibly. The **terracotta** look works particularly well on small objects such as the plastic urn which has been treated here.

When working this technique, it is best to use either water-based emulsions or acrylic paint colours. You will also need some sand, which you can pick up at your local home handyman store, and a rough, natural sea sponge.

Detailed or moulded items also look particularly attractive when finished with a terracotta effect, especially if they are going to be used in a conservatory or garden room. Protect the finish with a coat of oil-based varnish.

ABOVE: *The basic palette.*

1 Place the object on a newspaper or old sheet, then paint with the lighter colour.

2 While the paint is still wet, throw the dry builders' sand on to the wet surface, creating a random patchy finish.

3 Sponge patches of the darker colour over the object at random, making sure you leave some of the paler colour showing through.

4 Roughly sponge an orange, water-based paint on to the object. Leave to dry.

5 Mix up an off-white, water-based emulsion with 70 per cent water, and apply mix randomly over the plastic urn.

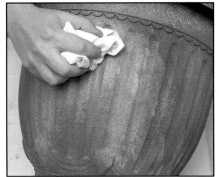

6 Rub any excess wash off with a rag, leaving enough to create a dusty look.

7 As an option, the aged look can be enhanced by sponging a turquoise blue colour over the urn.

LEAD

T HIS IS A PARTICULARLY good technique for adding visual weight to an object, giving it a much more solid appearance. This is a great paint technique when worked on displays and presentations since the surface always looks so much more solid and dense. The technique is often seen on display stands at exhibitions.

1 Paint the surface using a mid-grey water-based emulsion or acrylic paint and leave to dry.

2 Hold a silver spray can about 30 cm (12 in) from the surface and tap the top gently with a piece of wood. The paint will spatter out of the can in patches.

3 Mix up a black water-based emulsion with a little water and rub into some areas with a brush.

4 Mix up a wash of off-white emulsion using 60 per cent water and rub into the surface, blending it in in some areas.

LEFT : A plastic urn treated with the terracotta paint effect looks as effective as the real object.

ABOVE : A close-up of the lead paint effect shows how well this technique works on moulded areas.

RUST

THIS TECHNIQUE WORKS very well on garden ornaments where it would be found naturally, and is used on lamp bases in the home. It is often seen on seats, benches or ornaments for use in conservatories. Wherever the technique is found it has an almost theatrical, rich look.

Use water-based emulsions or acrylics to work the effect. Once again, the finished surface should be protected with a satin or matt oil-based varnish.

BELOW : The paint colours we used.

1 Apply a thick coat of water-based emulsion over the whole area. You can use any colour for this.

2 Immediately sprinkle sand over the thick coat of paint and leave the surface to dry completely.

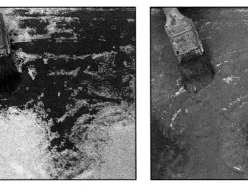

3 Using the dark brown colour, stipple and fitch the painted area, leaving some of the surface untouched by brown paint.

4 Fill in the remaining areas of the painted surface with the terracotta colour, again stippling and fitching the paint while you are working. Leave to dry.

5 Sprinkle the area with water, and stipple small areas of the surface with a blue-grey colour. Leave this to dry.

6 Again, sprinkle the area with water to ensure the paint will merge to give a more natural overall effect. Then spatter the area with orange paint.

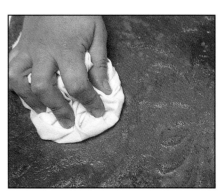

7 Using a rag, remove any excess water. Carefully merge some of the effects and leave to dry.

PEWTER

THIS IS ANOTHER TECHNIQUE which works well on small items, that may have been made from pewter in reality. Spray paints are ideal for creating this effect, but they must be used in well-ventilated areas and it is also a good idea to wear a mask.

To help the paint run smoothly, add some liquid detergent to the mixture.

1 *Spray or paint the object silver and leave to dry.*

2 *Fitch dark grey water-based emulsion or acrylic over the area and into any detailed mouldings.*

LEFT: The rust paint effect has been applied to an old piece of carved wood, transforming it into an attractive and stunning showpiece.

3 *Wipe off any excess paint with a soft rag.*

4 *Take a dry brush and rub the area hard to distress the remaining black paint into the silver surface.*

BELOW: Here are some examples of the different techniques you can achieve with paint and how effective these finishes can be on areas of raised and moulded details, such as embossed wallpapers.

5 *Add the finishing touches by spattering silver paint on with a toothbrush or by tapping the top of a silver spray can with a piece of wood.*

IMITATION GILDING

THIS IS A VERY POPULAR paint technique which can be used to give almost any object an embellished or highly gilded look, depending on the desired effect. The technique uses gold wax and fine tissue to create the effect, although it can be done in a variety of ways. This method is one of the simplest and cheapest and achieves good results time after time.

RIGHT: This is an example of how sumptuous and sophisticated gilding can look worked here in this small alcove.

1 *Paint or spray the object with a red oxide metal primer or a brown/red oil-based eggshell or undercoat.*

2 *While the paint is still wet, lay on several layers of fine tissue paper, overlapping and bunching the tissue paper as you lay it on to the object.*

3 *Using a brush and paint, flatten the tissue out, building up creases and crevices, and ensuring some tissue fits into recesses and moulding. Leave to dry.*

4 *Now apply the gold. Either use gold wax, spray paint or paint. One of the easiest ways to add gold is to rub on gold wax using a soft cloth.*

5 *Ensure the gold wax or paint covers the object and the moulded areas. Completely cover the object.*

6 *Rub the surface using a soft cloth. Using fine sandpaper, remove some gold paint to reveal the colour underneath.*

7 *Spatter some of the original colour on to the surface using an old brush and a piece of wood, then leave the paint to dry.*

METALLIC

A LUSTROUS METALLIC EFFECT can be achieved cheaply and effectively using proprietary spray paints. These must be used in a well-ventilated area, and you should also consider wearing a mask.

The idea is to build up layers of different coloured metallic car spray paints to achieve a sense of depth.

The colours can be sprayed in any order, but the last colour sprayed will usually be the predominant one. Try to avoid the spray going on to your skin by placing the hand which is holding the object into a polythene bag.

You can enhance the effect by adding a stencil motif on to the surface. Keep stencils in place with spray adhesive, which also helps stop the paint seeping under the stencil.

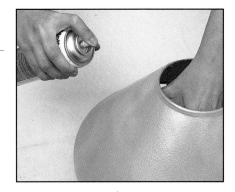

1 Holding the object securely, spray the first colour over it. Try to spray the paint fairly randomly.

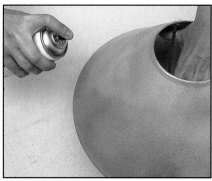

2 Using the next colour spray, coat the object randomly with this colour.

3 Add another colour, maintaining the random effect of colour.

4 Finally, spray the last colour over the object, remembering that this will be the predominant colour.

5 Add a finishing touch by spattering a darker oil-based colour on to the object.

6 The effect has been enhanced with a stencil stippled on to the surface using a gold wax paint.

7 Remove the acetate stencil before the gold paint has completely dried.

PROJECTS

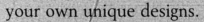

Using the techniques taught in
the previous section, here are a range of amazing decorative effects
created with paint.
Many of the techniques have been used in conjunction with each other
to maximize the options open to you and to show
how versatile each of the effects are. It is important to try to
use your own creativity when planning projects for your home. Use the ideas and
suggestions you find here as inspiration, and then create
your own unique designs.

MURAL

THIS MURAL WAS CREATED for a conservatory wall, where it adds three-dimensional interest and looks highly effective. The paint effect may look fairly daunting at first, but once it is broken down into simple stages, it is not difficult to achieve. All it takes is a little confidence, and a few everyday materials.

When attempting a project like this, try to incorporate any architectural features that already exist in the room into the paint effect. If there are none, you could add some features of your own. Here, for example, the dado rail and skirting board have been made to look like part of the stone wall.

You can add depth to the scene by varying the colours and sizes. The larger plants in the foreground add depth and help to enhance the finished look.

To create this mural, you need water-based paints in the basic colours given opposite. The first thing to do is to paint the whole surface in a mid-blue or cornflower blue water-based emulsion then leave the area to dry totally.

A good general hint when working on a scene or paint effect like this is to stand away from the painting occasionally so that you can check that you are creating the effect you had planned.

1 Wet the dry blue surface with water. Use a small brush to mark out the cloud shapes with a thinned white emulsion paint.

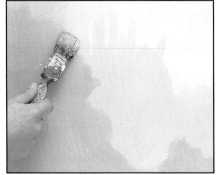

2 To create the three-dimensional effect, you need to soften some of the clouds using a soft dry brush and enhance the tips of others with white paint. Leave to dry.

3 Using a small brush, paint the first background silhouette using a light blue-green colour.

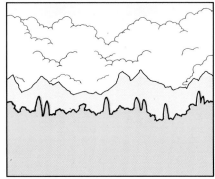

4 Repeat the process using a darker blue-green colour to enhance the background shapes. Paint the foreground trees using the same colour and leave the area to dry.

ABOVE: This is the rough cloud outline used here. Individualise it for your own scheme.

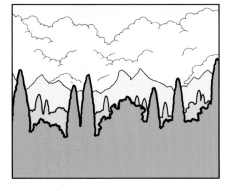

ABOVE: Use this pattern as the basis of the general background shapes worked here.

5 *To create a misty effect, apply a milky wash over the whole scene. Make up the milky wash with white emulsion thinned with 80 per cent water, then leave to dry.*

6 *Using a darker green paint, sponge on the foreground shapes. Use your imagination here to create hedges and arches.*

7 *Again using a sponge, add more interest to the foreground by painting flowers in bright colours: reds, yellows and oranges.*

8 *Using the same sponge, blend in the colours to soften the effect.*

LEFT : *The stonework has been made to look more realistic because the dado rail and the skirting boards have been incorporated.*

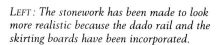

ABOVE : *The range of colours used to create the mural background.*

9 *Another method of painting the foreground is to use a feather. This will make unconventional marks. Finally, use stencils to create the border in the distance.*

Once you have reached this stage, you can transform the scene you have created into a view.

Some of the best scenes are seen through a window or a door, for example, but you could also consider creating an attractive trellis, which is the solution here. Painting a trellis gives you the opportunity to give even more of a three-dimensional effect to the scene by stencilling a trailing plant under and over the trellis.

RIGHT : A gothic door is one way of giving depth to the scene. For styles of architecture, consult books in the library.

BELOW : When painting a trellis it is best to paint the lines going in one direction first, then once dry, paint the opposite lines.

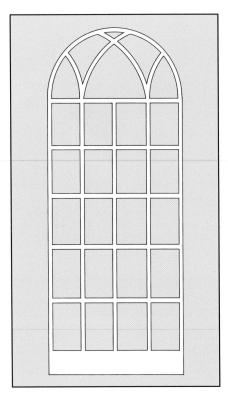

10 *Using the trellis design for reference, mark out the size of the trellis using a soft pencil and ruler. Check all your lines are straight.*

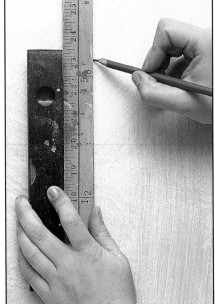

11 *To draw in the semi-circles, tie a pencil to a length of string and pin the string at the middle point of the circle. Pull against the string as you draw.*

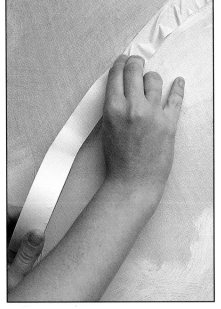

12 *Using low-tack masking tape, mask the areas so you can paint the semi-circle shape and vertical lines.*

13 *Paint in the lines using white water-based emulsion paint, and gently remove the masking tape while the paint is still wet. Leave to dry.*

14 *Once dry, mask off the diagonal trellis shapes, then paint with the white emulsion. Remove tape and again leave to dry.*

15 *Mask off the opposite diagonals, paint with white emulsion, remove the tape and leave to dry.*

ABOVE: *As an alternative, you can use a more advanced architectural arch. This arch looks out on to an imaginary landscape.*

Projects

16 *Use the template on page 93 to make a stencil from thin acetate. Apply spray adhesive and position. This leaves both hands free to paint.*

17 *Mix up a range of greens using olive green and terre verte. Add a little raw umber or white to darken or lighten the colours.*

18 *Using this range of colours, stencil a trailing effect over the trellis, building up some areas of foliage and leaving some parts almost bare.*

RIGHT: *Adding a trellis creates a different look and gives a totally new dimension to the garden room.*

19 Leave the stencilled leaves to dry, then add some stencilled flowers using primary colours mixed with raw umber or white to give different intensities.

20 Add some different flower shapes for some more contrast and variety.

21 Paint finishing touches by adding the suggestion of birds in the distance. Use a dark grey paint and a small brush and flick two lines to create the birds.

ABOVE: With practice and experience, the results from these simple steps can be totally stunning.

MURAL BASE

THERE ARE A NUMBER of effects which work well as the base for a mural. A marble or stone wall can be created easily, while brickwork is also effective. A stone or brick effect is created using a natural sponge and proprietary emulsions in the correct colours.

When working on the base, include the dado and skirting boards, since this makes the base look more solid.

ABOVE: Mix the stone colours using acrylic paint, or buy small cans of emulsion.

2 As the last colour you paint is generally predominant, finish the painting with the main stone colour.

1 Either use an old sea sponge or soften a new sponge by picking off any hard edges. Sponge the area at random using your chosen colours.

3 For the carved stone effect follow steps 10–13 on page 91.

RIGHT: This dining room is cleverly arranged so that wherever you sit you can look out through trompe l'oeil arches onto a landscaped garden.

4 Alternatively, create an old, red brickwork effect by roughly sponging on the colours given using a sponge.

5 Build up the effect by sponging on more red and terracotta colours, finishing with the final wall colour.

6 Once you are happy with the overall appearance, draw in the brickwork. Mark the horizontal lines using an off-white emulsion. Then fill in the verticals.

7 To make the brickwork look more effective, add some vertical lines which are not quite straight.

LEFT: *These are the colours used for brickwork.*

BLUE CABINET

CREATE A DISTRESSED, aged and washed out look on new furniture and wooden floors using a water-based emulsion. It will add interest to a piece which otherwise would have simply blended into the background. Either use the colours given here or experiment with different colours.

The cabinet and little shelving unit worked on here were made in softwood and MDF (medium density fibreboard).

1 *Rub down and smooth off any hard edges using a medium grade sandpaper.*

ABOVE : *The paint colours used for the cabinet.*

2 *If you are working with a new item, stain it with a strong coffee mix. This will show through on the finished piece and looks more authentic than new wood.*

3 *When dry, rub the raised areas and mouldings with furniture or candle wax. These areas will then resist subsequent layers of paint. Leave to dry.*

4 Thickly paint the object with the darker green colour. Leave to dry.

5 Rub the paint off in some areas using a medium grade sandpaper to expose some of the stained wood underneath.

6 Thin the lighter coloured paint with about 40 per cent water and coat the object with this paint mixture, covering the mouldings and recesses.

7 Before the paint has dried, use a soft rag to remove any excess paint and create a distressed look.

ABOVE : The same effect has been used on the dresser in this room.

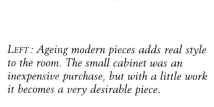

LEFT : Ageing modern pieces adds real style to the room. The small cabinet was an inexpensive purchase, but with a little work it becomes a very desirable piece.

8 Apply an off-white wash, made with white emulsion and 50 per cent water over the whole surface, rubbing into the recesses and mouldings. Leave to dry.

9 Using a medium grade sandpaper, reveal more of the underlying colour and stained wood. Work carefully at this stage.

10 Once you are happy with the effect, apply a coat of oil-based varnish tinted with a little raw umber.

'ANTIQUE' MAHOGANY CHESS BOARD

Make the most of old and unused items around the home, especially when you first start playing with paint techniques. Here, an old tool box, which was found at the back of a garage, has been given a totally new lease of life.

Firstly, the box was painted with a mahogany paint finish, and then a chess grid was added to its top surface. The interior of the box now holds the chess pieces. The same technique could also be applied to an old table.

1 Coat the surface with an oil-based salmon-pink paint. Mark out the pattern using the diagram. At this stage, ignore the striped effect around the edges.

2 The two predominant colours are burnt sienna and burnt umber. Mix in a little oil-based varnish into the colours, then brush them on to the surface carefully.

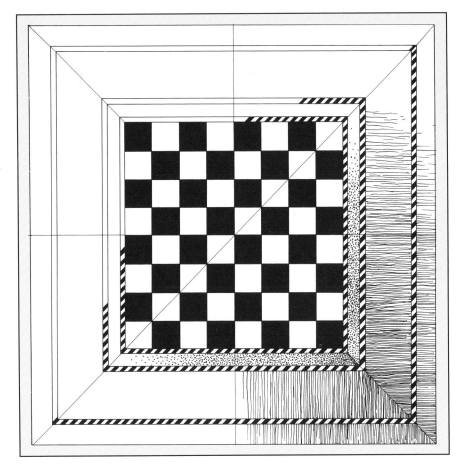

3 Drag a small brush through the glaze to give a grained effect. Soften using a soft pasting brush, thus giving the illusion of depth.

LEFT: The chessboard. If necessary this diagram can be blown up on a photocopier to fit the size of table you are going to work. Alternatively, simply enlarge the design as you mark it out.

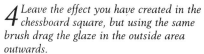

4 *Leave the effect you have created in the chessboard square, but using the same brush drag the glaze in the outside area outwards.*

5 *To achieve the mitred corner, use a piece of card across the corner you are painting.*

6 *Carefully stipple the area between the edge and the chessboard using a small stippling brush. Leave the surface to dry.*

7 *Now work on the chessboard itself. Using a low-tack masking tape, mask off the areas around the squares and fill in the areas with black paint.*

LEFT: *Using paint, you can create amazing finishes. The board here has a mahogany look that was created with paint, then treated with black paint to create the chequerboard design.*

The main aim of this piece of work was to create an individual item, not to recreate photographically a mahogany finish (although to create the mahogany finish a piece of wood was used for design guidance).

The trick is to try and emulate the general characteristics of the mahogany wood, and give the box a new purpose by adding a chessboard.

Although mahogany wood was used as the background for this chess set, you may prefer to work the design over a different paint finish. Ragging or dragging could work well, but it would be better to avoid a busy effect, which could detract from the design.

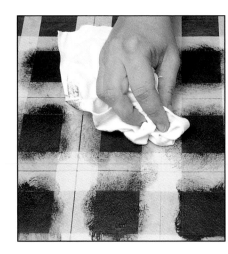

8 Rag off the excess black paint to reveal some of the graining underneath.

9 Before the paint has completely dried, gently remove the masking tape and repeat filling in the remaining squares.

RIGHT: *When the box is not in use for playing chess it can be used as a small side or coffee table.*

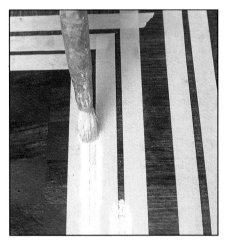

11 *Paint these lines with a dirty-looking off-white paint and leave to dry.*

10 *Once all the black paint has dried, mask off the lines which frame each differently painted section. Mark off lines of about 5mm (¼in) all round.*

12 *Use a small brush to paint on diagonal black lines, then carefully remove the masking tape and leave the paint to dry.*

13 *Finally, apply two coats of gloss varnish tinted with a small amount of burnt sienna.*

BOXES

SMALLER OBJECTS RESPOND well to the many different paint techniques. They also offer a good opportunity to experiment and try out some of the more unusual paint effects.

Here, a selection of boxes have been treated to a range of different finishes. Some of the effects have also been enhanced with trims, such as gold painted lines or little stencil designs.

ABOVE: This jewellery box has been painted using a malachite-inspired paint effect (see page 38). This has been enhanced with lines of gold paint.

ABOVE: The lapis lazuli paint effect (see page 39) has transformed all the small boxes and the table top. Gold paint adds the finishing touch.

RIGHT: All the boxes and objects in this picture look expensive and exclusive, but in reality they are all painted using a variety of techniques.

ABOVE: The tortoiseshell paint technique worked in different ways gives a whole range of possible effects.

ABOVE: The tortoiseshell effect (see page 36) painted here has been enhanced using gold paint.

ABOVE: Here, a grained wood panelled effect has been created using wood colours like burnt sienna and burnt umber.

CHILDREN'S ROOMS

F OR AN EFFECTIVE LOOK in a child's bedroom, it is best to take a theme and work around it, even to the extent of painting boxes, cupboards and furniture using the same design. However, when working on children's rooms, ensure you use a theme which can grow with the child, unless you intend changing the scheme regularly.

The rooms here have been inspired by various stories from books and age-old, traditional and popular themes. You can also get ideas and inspiration from children's wallpaper or fabric designs.

RIGHT: Give interest to a plain wall by painting a simple roller blind on to a sponged background.

ABOVE: The wardrobe unit has been transformed into a rustic oak-beamed cottage with foliage around the base.

RIGHT: The whole room has been treated using simple paint techniques, and gives the overall impression of an overgrown garden.

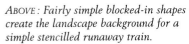

ABOVE: Fairly simple blocked-in shapes create the landscape background for a simple stencilled runaway train.

ABOVE: A cloud shape cut from MDF (medium density fibreboard) echoes the clouds painted on the walls.

ABOVE: A simple mural transforms an ordinary built-in wardrobe and drawers.

DUCK BEDROOM

PAINT THE WALL in a bright, sunny yellow, water-based emulsion paint. Using the duck templates given on page 97, make a couple of stencils in two different sizes, small and medium.

Use these stencils to decorate the walls with painted ducks, following the instructions below. The theme was taken a stage further in this bedroom as the duck shape has also been used to make the duck headboard, which has been cut out from MDF (medium density fibreboard) then painted.

1 Stencil the medium-sized duck around the room (see page 97). Colour the body in. Then make a smaller stencil and paint the smaller duck in the spaces.

2 Using a much smaller paint brush, fill in the beaks and eyes on all the ducks.

3 Using the small brush, fill in the wings working freehand.

4 If there is no dado rail, draw a line about 76 cm (30 in) above the floor and paint the first wave outline along this line. Paint in the area below the wave.

5 Now paint further waves freehand with a small paintbrush, or use the stencil given on page 97.

LEFT: The inspiration behind this stencilled bedroom came from a discontinued wallpaper, and the design has been taken a stage further with the addition of smaller ducks.

6 Draw and cut out various nautical shapes such as shells, seahorses and shellfish from acetate or card, and stencil them in a dark blue or gold in the painted section below the waves.

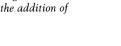

CAROUSEL

THIS IS ANOTHER good theme for a child's room, and again is it fairly quick and easy to create. Although the finished effect may look rather complicated, it is simply a matter of taking each step at a time.

After the tented effect has been painted, use the stencils given on page 96 to fill in the design. The room can be painted with water-based emulsion paints.

Firstly, tack a long piece of string to the centre of the ceiling, and using this as a guide, draw lines to the four corners of the room. Then draw lines to the middle point between the ceiling and the wall, and break each section up twice more. Now create the inner circle. Tie a pencil about 50 cm (20 in) from the centre and using this as a compass, draw the inner circle. Working around the inner circle and following the lines already drawn, draw in two scalloped shapes in the inner circle.

Work the outer scallops. Using a pencil and a ruler, follow the drawn lines down the walls for about 60 cm (24 in) and use a large plate to draw in the scalloped edges. Lastly, draw in the final scallops under the tented area freehand.

Once all the areas are drawn in, the tented area can be painted. Choose colours to suit the scheme for the room.

1 Draw straight lines down from the tented ceiling, stopping them at different heights. Then stick the rope stencil (page 96) at the end of one of these lines.

2 Stencil the first colour of the rope, using the pencil lines as a guide. Leave the paint to dry.

3 Add interest to the rope section by stencilling a second and even a third colour to the rope.

4 Position the horse stencil given on page 96 at the end of one rope section.

5 Fill in the main body of the horse using one colour of paint, and leave to dry.

6 Fill in the details using different colours of paint. When you are working this design, it is important to wait for the paint to dry before adding a second colour.

7 Repeat the process for all the other lengths of rope.

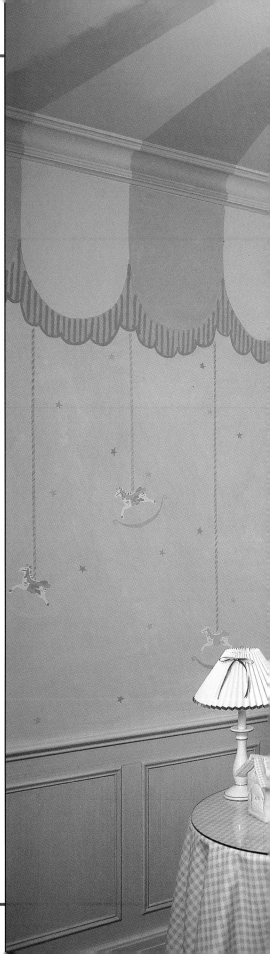

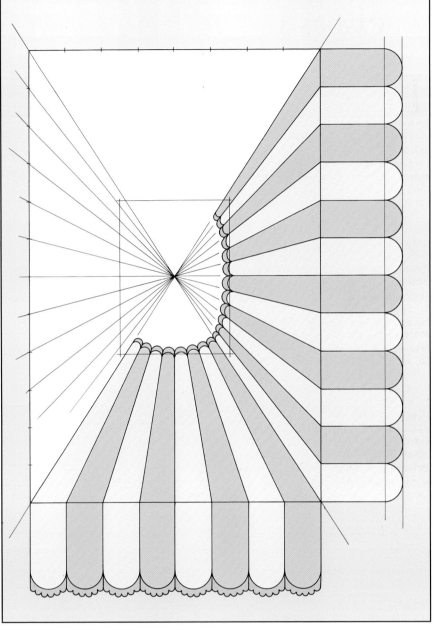

LEFT : *Dancing horses add real movement to this child's bedroom. It is just the room most children would love to own. The overall effect has been enhanced with a toy rocking horse placed on the bedside table.*

ABOVE : *The tented ceiling design, which could be painted in a range of colours. Here, pastels are used.*

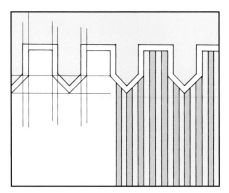

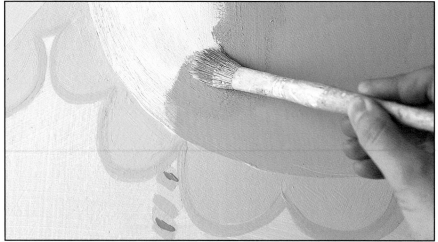

ABOVE and BELOW: The diagrams offer different alternative edgings to the tented ceiling, both of which are fairly easy to follow.

1 Block in the colour on the tented ceiling using a fairly large brush.

2 Pick out areas of detail using a much smaller, finer brush.

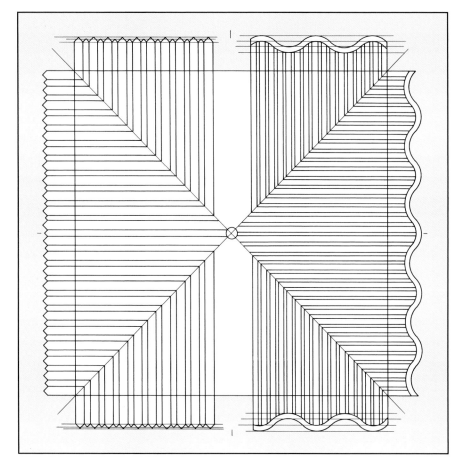

3 This is the finished tented effect before the ropes are stencilled.

LEFT: The carousel painted here is worked in exactly the same way as the one on the previous page, but different colour, and motifs have been used.

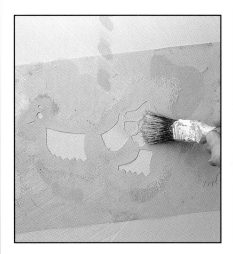

ABOVE: Position the stencil with spray adhesive, then paint in the designs letting each colour dry before adding the next.

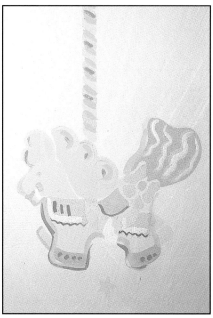

ABOVE: The inspiration behind these animals was taken from a wallpaper border and then transferred to stencils.

ABOVE: A cute and colourful motif works well such as the little elephant design which has been used here.

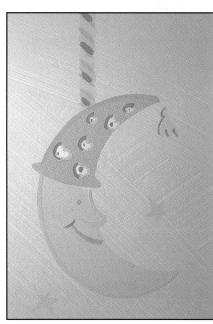

ABOVE: The man in the moon, a particularly simple and effective design motif.

STENCIL MOTIFS

STENCILLING IS A FAIRLY cheap and very versatile method of enhancing any surface, and there are many simple and effective ways to alter the stencilled image to improve the overall effect.

Purchased stencils are fine, but for more personal images and creative looks, use different and unusual images.

Paintings by renaissance artists like Mantegna (1431 – 1506) are a wonderful source of inspiration for borders and motifs when stencilling. Look at books in your local library for ideas.

Almost any image from a fabric, a book or a piece of china can be used as inspiration and source material for stencilling. Find the image you like and copy it on to tracing paper, or photocopy and enlarge or reduce the image to the required size. Transfer this image on to stencil card or acetate film and cut around the image using a craft knife, remembering to leave any bridging pieces intact so that the image will hold together.

It is best to spray the back of your stencil with spray adhesive, which can be bought from most art shops. This low-tack spray allows you to stick the stencil to the wall or object, leaving both hands free to paint. It also helps to prevent the paint from bleeding under the edges, avoiding any fuzzy shapes. Because the spray glue is low-tack, the stencil can be easily moved.

1 Spray the back of the stencil, position it carefully, then stipple the first colour using a fairly stiff brush and water-based paints.

2 Remove the stencil to reveal a sharp image and leave to dry.

3 Reposition the same stencil over the image, but move it slightly to one side and stencil again with an off-white paint.

4 Remove the stencil to reveal a more three-dimensional effect and leave to dry.

*LEFT : The stencil design used to enhance
and embellish this Victorian fireplace. The
design was inspired by a detail on a
painting by Andrea Mantegna.*

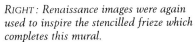

*RIGHT : Renaissance images were again
used to inspire the stencilled frieze which
completes this mural.*

*ABOVE : The image used here was
influenced by the design on the fabrics
found in the room, which enhances the
overall effect.*

*LEFT : The candle sconce here neatly echoes
the damask stencil which has been used on
the next page.*

83

DAMASK ROOM

THE WONDERFUL stencil designs in this room were inspired by an expensive Warners fabric which has been used for the curtains. Although this project looks sumptuous, and somewhat ambitious, it is not too difficult to realise. The effect works particularly well in this room with its high ceiling and deep cornice.

Here, the image was easily translated from the fabric. However, if you can't find an image you want to use as a stencil, you could use one of the ones provided on pages 92-97 or at the back of the book.

1 Thin a water-based paint with about 50 per cent water and apply this over the background area.

2 Rag or distress the area with a rag or a dry brush to create a soft background as the base for your stencil. Leave to dry.

3 Use a plumbline (a weight tied to a piece of string will do the trick) to position the stencil on the wall. Stencil the main colour using a water-based emulsion.

4 Use a soft rag to remove any excess paint and distress the image slightly.

5 Sponge the darker colour at random to break up the image a little, then remove the stencil.

RIGHT: *This is a good example of how sophisticated stencilling can look when used with the right image in appropriate surroundings.*

6 Once the image is dry, enhance the distressed look by rubbing the paint lightly with a fine grade sandpaper.

7 Sponge an off-white emulsion paint over the stencil to soften the image.

8 Apply a milky wash, made up with off-white emulsion and about 70 per cent water, over the whole area and distress with a dry brush.

9 Carefully rub off patches of the milky wash to expose some sharper areas of the stencil.

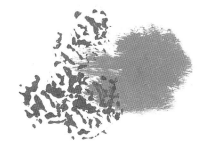

LEFT: *The main paint colours which were used in this room.*

STENCILLED SCREEN

A SCREEN OR ROOM divider can easily be made to any size using pre-cut MDF (medium density fibreboard) boards, which are then hinged together. Most timber merchants will cut fibreboards to the required size.

If you wish to individualize the screen, why not try shaping the top with a domed or rounded shape, or even design a castle or crenellated shape?

The stencils used here have been given on pages 92 and 94, but you could create your own design using different stencils, either ready-made or hand-made ones. If you do create your own design, try it out on a piece of card before painting the screen itself. Your final design or the design used here could also be applied to a panel or a door in the home.

Before you start to work on the screen, you need to prepare it. Coat the fibreboard with a proprietary wood primer, then apply two coats of oil-based white eggshell.

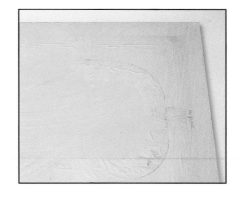

1 On a colour washed background, mask off the corner and border areas.

2 Stipple on the first colour between the masked off areas.

3 Carefully remove the masking tape.

4 Mask off the middle panels and apply a water-based emulsion thinned with 40 per cent water.

5 Rag inside this panel to create a cloudy effect. Leave to dry.

6 Using a fine brush, paint grey lines around the border and corner shapes.

7 Use the template on page 92 to make a stencil for the corner design. Stencil the corner designs.

8 Use the corner stencil to stencil a design along the edges. Leave to dry.

9 Use the template on page 94 to make the central design, and position the stencil.

10 Using a small brush, stipple different colours on to the stencil, blending areas to add interest.

11 Carefully remove the stencil to reveal the central design underneath.

12 Use the garland template on page 94 to stencil over the panels and pull the design together.

LEFT: *Once you are happy with the design, make the painting more durable by covering it with two layers of oil-based varnish.*

SCREEN REVERSE

THE EFFECT CREATED on the reverse of this screen uses the central stencil from the previous screen seen on pages 86–87, but has a totally different look. This is due to the fact that more dramatic bolder colours have been used. Again, the effect could be created on a door or panel if you prefer.

1 Apply a glaze and rag the whole area to create an interesting working background.

2 Using a low-tack masking tape, mask off a panel 5 cm (2 in) from the edge and apply a wash of artists' oil-based Prussian blue mixed with a little oil-based varnish.

3 Using a very soft rag, rag this wash to create a soft, cloudy effect.

4 Carefully remove the masking tape to show a straight edge, and leave the screen to dry.

5 *Using a low-tack masking tape, mask off an area 5cm (2in) inside the blue panel, and use a cup to draw in the quarter circles in the corners.*

6 *Using a low-tack masking tape, mask off these quarter circles.*

7 *Apply a clear varnish mixed with a little turpentine to the area which has been masked off.*

8 *While the varnish is still wet, use a toothbrush to spatter gold paint mixed with a little turpentine on to the surface. Leave the screen to dry.*

9 *Contain this panel by painting a fine gold line around the edge using a fine artists' paintbrush.*

LEFT : *The final screen looks very dramatic. This is really due to the use of much bolder colours in comparison to the previous page.*

RIGHT : *This is a good example of how a hand-painted screen can be used in a sophisticated dining room.*

10 *Use a ruler and a fine paintbrush to paint a fine white line around around the outside edge.*

11 *Use the template on page 94 to make up the central stencil. Use this to stencil the design in the centre of the panel, stippling with a gold paint.*

TROMPE L'OEIL PANELLING

W HEN PRESENTED with the main picture, very few people believe that the panels below the dado rail have been created with paint alone. This is, however, the case, and this room offers an extremely good example of how convincing and effective a *trompe l'oeil* panel can be.

Once again, one of the tricks which makes the paint effect so convincing is the fact that the dado rail and skirting board have been incorporated in the design.

Before you start to paint, check the dimensions of the panels and scale them up or down to fit the area you are going to be working.

1 Create a highly dragged surface using an oil-based oatmeal eggshell paint. Leave to dry, then mark out the panels following the diagram.

2 Mix artists' oil colours, raw umber, raw sienna and burnt umber with glaze. Apply and drag vertically across the areas inside the panels and verticals between.

3 Drag and comb down this area to create a random combed effect in some parts of the panel.

4 Use a heartgrainer to create a heartgrained effect elsewhere in the panel area.

5 Using a homemade comb from stiff card, fill in any other areas in the panel.

6 Finally, enhance all the effects by lightly dragging the comb over the panel area again.

7 Soften the combed and grained effect you have created in some areas with a soft dusting brush worked lightly into the surface.

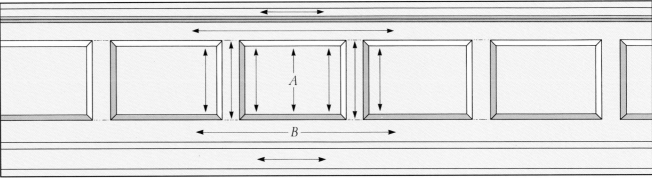

ABOVE : Firstly, work the inner verticals A, then the horizontal areas above and below the panels B.

RIGHT: These panels have been created with the simple use of paint. This is a good way of showing just how effective *trompe l'oeil* panelling can be.

8 Now work the horizontal areas above and below the panels. Brush the same colour on to this area.

9 Using the comb, heartgrainer and dusting brush, create a wooden effect, but work horizontally. Once you are happy with this, leave the surface to dry.

10 Create highlights by painting a thin off-white wash between the previously drawn pencil lines on the top and down one side.

11 Create shadows by painting raw umber mixed with a little varnish between the bottom lines and remaining sides. Leave to dry.

12 Enhance the three-dimensional look further by reinforcing the highlights. Paint small fine lines using a small brush and a ruler.

13 Strengthen the shadows by painting a darker line, again with raw umber, along the shadow edge.

TEMPLATES

The following pages present the stencil designs which have been used throughout Part One of the book, or have been included because they offer extra inspiration to the reader. All the designs can be sized up or down on a photocopier depending on the area they are to be used for.

CORNER STENCIL This could be used for many projects, from floorcloths to screens and even furniture.

SCROLL STENCIL The design for this stencil was inspired by the work of Mantegna, and has been used throughout Part One.

FLORAL CORNER This stencil has been used for the screen on pages 86-89. It would work well as a corner design on a wall or elsewhere around the home.

DISPLAY TIME A good stencil for anywhere around the home.

CENTRAL STENCIL This stencil has been used for the mural on pages 58-63, and could also be used as a border or frieze.

SCREEN STENCIL This stencil has been used
for the screen on pages 86-89, but would also work
well as a border.

EDGING This stencil has been used for the screen
on pages 86-87, but could also be used as a border.

FINE ART A border which could be used on walls
or furniture around the home.

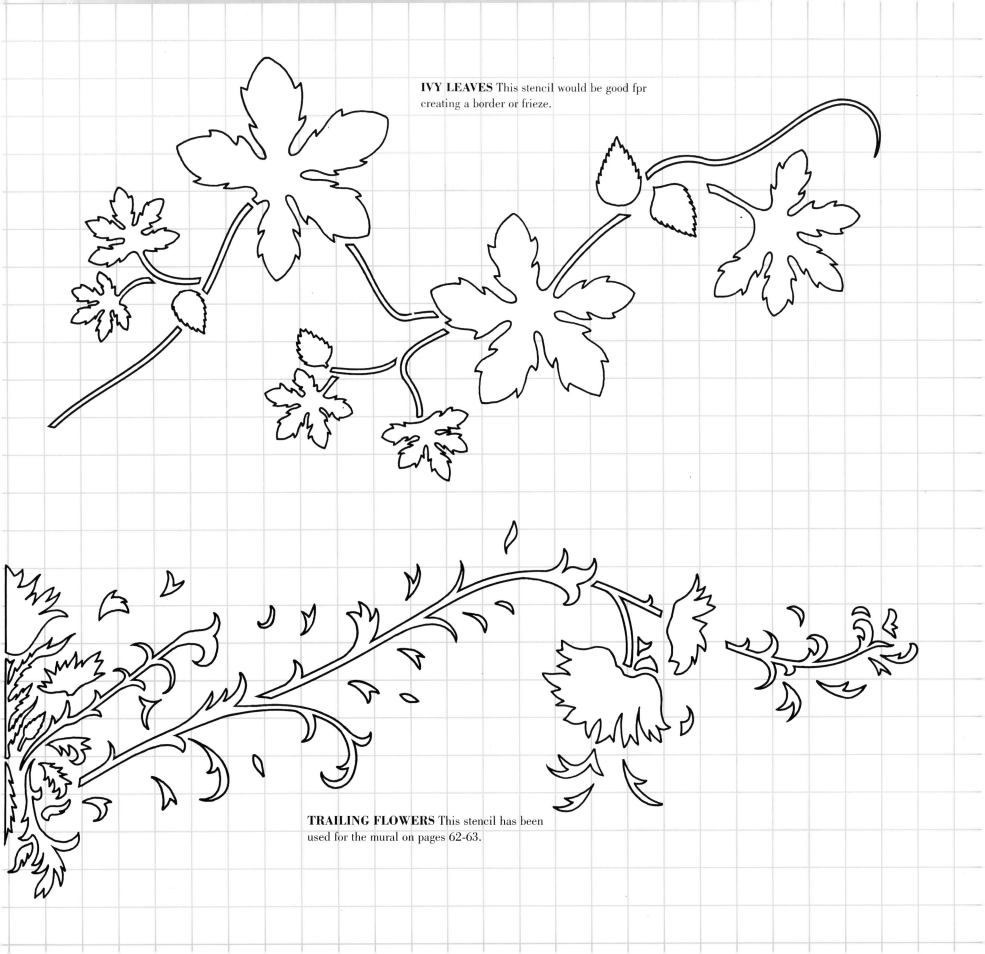

IVY LEAVES This stencil would be good fpr creating a border or frieze.

TRAILING FLOWERS This stencil has been used for the mural on pages 62-63.

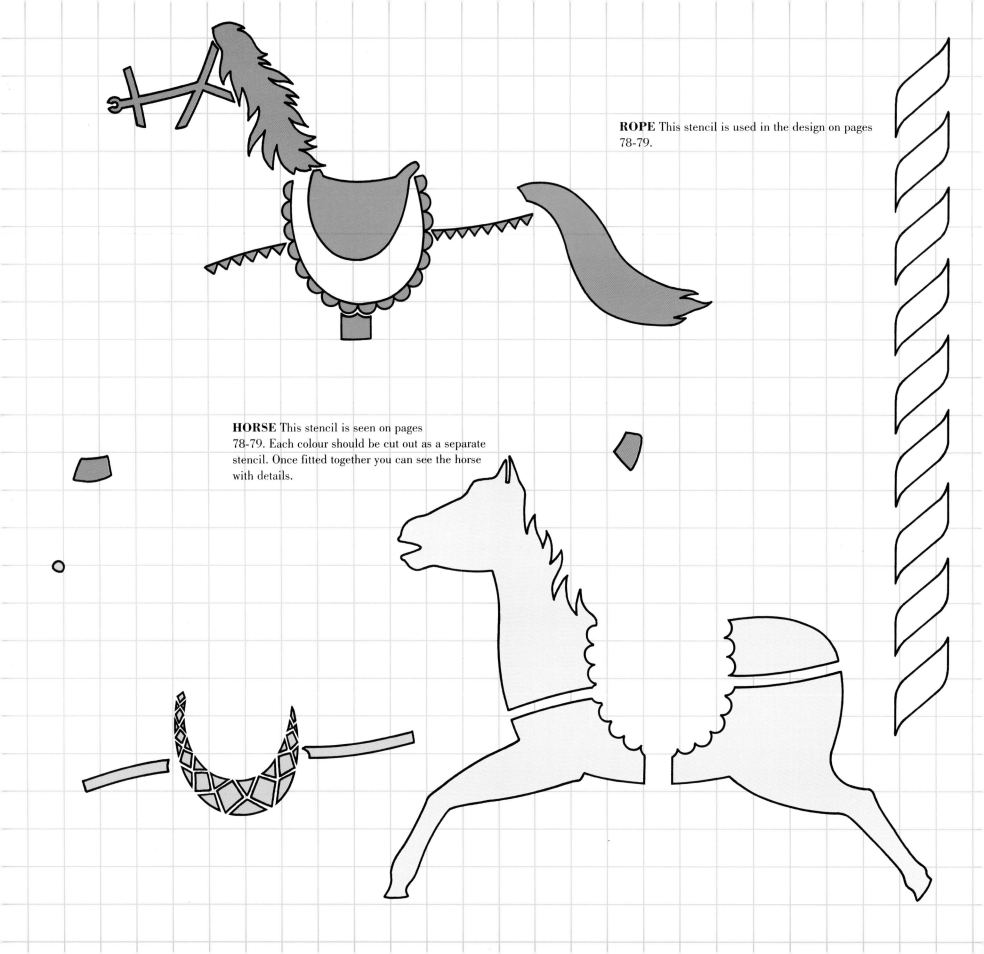

ROPE This stencil is used in the design on pages 78-79.

HORSE This stencil is seen on pages 78-79. Each colour should be cut out as a separate stencil. Once fitted together you can see the horse with details.

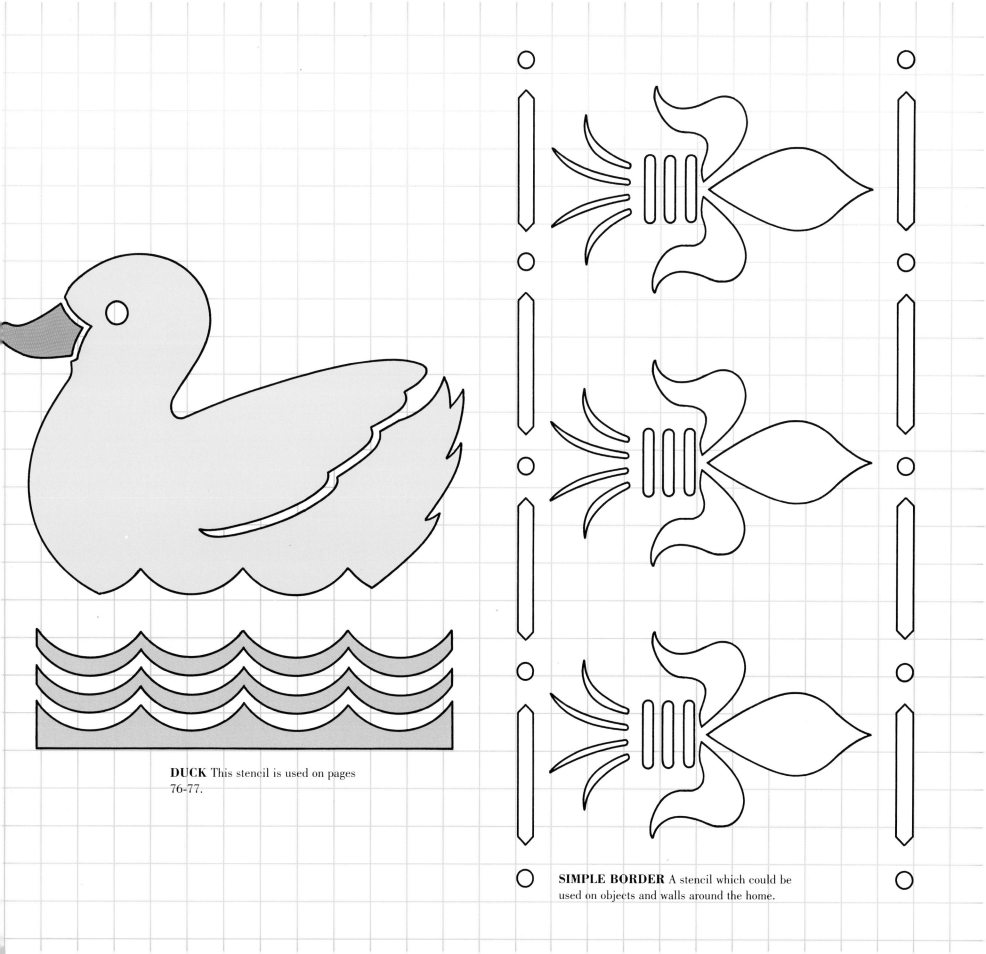

DUCK This stencil is used on pages 76-77.

SIMPLE BORDER A stencil which could be used on objects and walls around the home.

PART TWO
Stencilling

MATERIALS &
EQUIPMENT

Preparing for stencilling

Before you can start the process of stencilling, you must have something to stencil on! This section shows you how to prepare a variety of items using materials readily available from do-it-yourself or art stores.

Old furniture is best stripped and then painted or left with a natural wood surface. Strip off any old finish with **paint** or **varnish remover**, wearing **protective gloves**. Otherwise, engage a professional stripper, who will use either acid or a non-caustic stripper.

Sand your wood or metal smooth with **steel wool** or **sandpaper**, both available in three basic grades. Fill holes and cracks with **fine surface filler** for wood or **car body filler** for metal.

Repair wood with **quick-drying glue**. **PVA** (polyvinyl acetate) **medium** is a versatile, non-toxic glue that can be used for sticking paper and fabric.

Invest in a couple of good quality **paint** and **artist's brushes**. Use **turpentine** to clean your brushes after using oil-based paints like gloss and eggshell. For a few of the projects you may need some more unusual sounding items such as **acrylic gesso** (from art stores) to make grainy wood seem smooth, **a steel rule** or a **heartgrainer** to simulate the grain lines of wood. Occasionally, a **jigsaw** is needed to cut holes in the centre of a wooden sheet, but if you prefer you can ask a local carpenter to do this for you.

In addition, it is a good idea to save **newspapers**, **glass jars** with lids, **plastic containers** and **old rags**, all of which you will need for these projects.

Cutting a stencil

Stencilling is achieved by applying paint through holes cut in either **oiled Manilla card** or **plastic film**. Craft suppliers and good art stores stock card in sizes 38 x 51 cm (15 x 20 in) and 51 x 76 cm (20 x 30 in). It is ready for use, having been 'oiled' in manufacture. Plastic film comes in numerous shapes and sizes, generally on the small side, in clear, blue and opaque white varieties. It has the great advantage of being see-through, but is costly and harder to cut than the card.

To mark your design on card, use a sharp **2B pencil** or **permanent marker pen**. To copy a template from the back of the book, use **tracing paper** and **typist's carbon** (available from stationers). Very large sheets of **dressmaker's carbon** made can be bought at haberdashers.

To cut a stencil in either card or film, use a sharp **craft knife,** but nothing too heavy or with a bulky handle. The scalpel shown here has **removable blades**, sold in packets of five in stationers and art stores.

Stencilling

Keeping your stencil firmly in place while you are applying the colour is essential. Use **spray adhesive** (from art stores), which, although tacky enough to adhere the stencil to any clean, dry surface, enables you to peel the stencil off without leaving any residual glue, and to reposition it again and again before respraying. For an intricate stencil it is really unbeatable, but **masking tape** stuck all around the outer edge of the card or film will suffice as long as care is taken not to lift up any delicate parts of the stencil while working.

Liquid stencil paints are available in small quantities (but go a long, long, way) and in a wide range of colours. There are two kinds. **Hard-surface paints** are exactly that, for use on firm surfaces such as walls and furniture, while **fabric paints** are for textiles. **Oil-based crayons** come in a limited range of colours. They need cleaning from time to time with **turpentine**.

Stencil brush sizes start at 5 mm (³⁄₁₆ in) and go up to several centimetres (approximately 1½ in) across. Try to have a separate brush for each colour. Wash them clean with **cellulose thinners** (available from car accessory stores) as soon as you have finished using them to extend their useful life.

Finishing

Your object for stencilling does not have to have a plain, painted colour as a base. Make it more interesting by trying some of the simple paint techniques suggested in the projects to add interest and texture underneath your motifs. 'Dragging' with a specialist **dragging brush** – or a **wallpaper brush** – produces a series of soft lines. Sponging (use a **natural sponge** only) gives a more textured effect. Try your hand at reproducing the effect of liming, but only on areas not to be stencilled, or colour wood in unusual shades before you start your stencilling.

After all your hard work in preparation and stencilling, protect your work with a coat of **varnish** if possible. On furniture, use a polyurethane **varnish** in a choice of matt, satin or gloss. Protect tiles with special **ceramic varnish**. An interesting kind of varnish available from art stores, **crackle glaze**, will give your model an 'antique' effect. Different manufacturers produce crackle glazes that vary in technique so read the instructions carefully before starting. In general, it is a two-part varnish which, when left to dry, leaves small or large cracks on the surface that can be coloured with thinned artist's oil paint to produce the antique effect.

Cleaning

Do not attempt to clean an area of stencilling with anything stronger than a **damp cloth** and a little **liquid detergent**. Do not rub or soak your newly painted model or you will damage the paint (though sometimes worn paint can look old and interesting).

If stencilling on glass with stencil paints, it will be necessary to paint on a coat of protective varnish to enable thorough cleaning. When cleaning glass, test an inconspicuous area first with a stick wrapped in cotton wool. Do not use window cleaning fluids.

TECHNIQUES

THE SAME BASIC techniques occur in many of the projects used in Part Two. Before starting any project, it is important that you take the time to read through the techniques needed and to practise the methods used.

Prepare your surface thoroughly before beginning stencilling. Follow the cutting techniques carefully to ensure that your stencils last for a long time and start by using the recommended stencilling technique for each project. With time and more experience, you will be able to make your own decisions about paints and techniques. Finally, do not worry if you make a mistake by smudging the stencil since this can be remedied with the right materials.

Stripping wood

Preparation is all important to a good finish. Remove old paint or varnish, stripping by hand with a stripping agent (always protect your hands with rubber gloves), or send to a professional stripper. On flat surfaces, use a metal scraper to remove the worst of the surface. On curves and to reach into crevices, apply stripper on a brush and remove using steel wool.

Preparing wood

After stripping, the object will need sanding to achieve a smooth surface on which to apply your chosen finish. Use various grades of glasspaper or steel wool, coarse first, then medium, then finish with fine. Before painting, brush down with a dry paintbrush and wipe with a clean rag dampened in turpentine. This lifts off any dust and dries quickly.

Applying paint

Paints are divided between water- or oil-based types. Water-based paints are emulsions and acrylics, which dry quickly and can be cleaned with water. Oil-based paints are gloss and eggshell. They dry much more slowly and need to be cleaned with turpentine. Self-undercoating and eggshell varieties can be painted straight onto prepared wood.

Detailing by hand

The two stencils used for this cat's head, body and feature markings would, stencilled alone, result in a rather crude image. By adding details, a very realistic picture can be achieved. Here, a photograph has been used for reference. The head and body have been coloured to resemble the photograph, with the features and markings in appropriate colours. An artist's brush has then been used to outline and highlight the eyes and to add whiskers and hairs.

Marbling

1 Remove any finish or varnish and sand smooth with glasspaper or steel wool (see opposite). Paint with two coats of white eggshell. Allow to dry. Mix two glazes (see page 105). Dampen a natural sponge with turpentine, squeeze out any excess and dip into one glaze. Dab randomly all over the surface. Clean the sponge with turpentine and warm, soapy water. Repeat with the second glaze. When marbling, do not stop between steps, not even to make a coffee. You must not let the glazes dry out!

2 To soften the dappling effect of sponging, lightly flick all over with the softening brush to blend the two shades of glaze. (Alternatively, use a good quality paintbrush with thick, tightly-packed bristles.) Soak a clean rag in turpentine and use to wipe any excess paint from the bristles of the softening brush. Do this several times while you work.

3 Soak a small piece of clean rag in turpentine and wring out any excess. Roll the rag up, making sure there are creases in it. Gently roll it over the entire surface, slightly changing direction all the time. Wash it out in more turpentine to clean, or use a new piece once it becomes covered in paint. This technique lifts the glaze off in varying degrees.

4 Mix three glazes for painting in the veining. Mix the darkest one from artist's oil paints (viridian and raw umber) and turpentine only. Mix two further shades of glaze adding cadmium yellow to veridian in two different strengths. Use a separate artist's brush for each glaze, one thin, one larger and one square-ended, to add variation and width to the veins. Paint veins in all over. Twist the brush as you work to vary the line and overlap the two colours.

5 Brush over the veining with the softening brush, using a light flicking movement. Flick in one direction only as this is how veining occurs naturally. The 'softening' should merge all the colours and blend the veins into the background in some places and not in others. Leave to dry. If you do not like the effect, wipe off with turpentine and start again.

Verdigris

1 Place the article on several layers of newspaper in a well-ventilated area and spray with a can of copper-coloured paint. Repeat several times for an even finish. In a glass jar, pour a little dark emerald green matt emulsion paint. Dilute 2:1 with water. Paint over the copper – it will not cover evenly – and allow to dry.

2 Using a separate brush for each colour, dab on the three verdigris pastes (see opposite) at random over the article. Do not quite cover the emerald green emulsion. Store any remaining paste with a lid on. The paste will keep for a few weeks. Thin if necessary with methylated spirits.

3 Do not stop for a break between the stages of applying the pastes. The verdigris needs to be kept damp. Carefully spoon some of the whiting into a cooking sieve and gently rub it through the mesh with the underside of the spoon so that it coats the wet verdigris pastes.

4 With a household paintbrush, flick over the entire surface of the frame to remove any excess whiting. Using the same brush dipped in clean water, wash over the whole frame to slightly dampen it. This will 'set' the whiting and blend it with the pastes.

5 Continue working without breaking off so the whiting does not dry. Gently rub over the complete frame with medium or fine grade steel wool. The aim is to leave patches of the pastes intact, to allow the emerald emulsion to show through and also to rub through to the copper layer. The ingredients used in this method of verdigris will not withstand being left outdoors.

Verdigris paste

1 Take three glass bowls and place four or five spoonfuls of whiting into each (whiting is a dry, plaster-like substance, available from specialist decorating stores). Buy small sample pots of matt emulsion paint in two shades of minty green and one shade of pale blue.

2 Add some blue emulsion to one of the bowls and mix thoroughly with an artist's paintbrush to form a dry paste. Thin with methylated spirits until the paste becomes the consistency of thick double cream. Repeat in the two remaining bowls with the two shades of green emulsion, using a separate brush for each colour.

Mixing glazes

Glazes are thin washes of coloured paint, generally pale shades, applied over a base coat that then still shows through. Ready-made glazes are available from specialist paint firms.

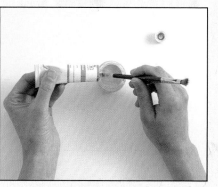

1 Pour a little white eggshell paint into a glass jar and add artist's oil colour (or any coloured oil-based paint) bit by bit, mixing together thoroughly with a brush before adding more colour. If the colour seems too deep, add more white eggshell or preferably another artist's oil paint to lighten and create an individual shade.

2 Thin the glaze with turpentine, adding a little at a time and mixing it in thoroughly, until you have the consistency of thin cream. Store with the lid firmly closed. Should you leave the glaze for some time before using, it may thicken slightly. Add turpentine to thin. Darker tones of glaze can be made, thinning oil-based paint or artist's oils with turpentine only (do not add white eggshell). These have a tendency to dry out and ought to be used immediately.

Making and cutting stencils

Stencils for the projects in Part Two should be cut from oiled Manilla card unless otherwise specified.

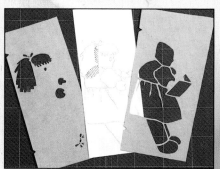

1 Trace templates directly onto plastic film using a fine marker pen. For Manilla card, trace the template onto tracing paper. Trace over these outlines onto stencil card, inserting typing carbon in between. Where two or more stencils are needed to complete an image, trace and cut the main outline from one piece of card, then cut any details onto one or more pieces of card. The body and head of this cat were cut on one stencil, its eyes, nose and markings on another.

2 Cut around the outlines of the design. To cut any stencil, no matter how simple, you will require a sharp craft knife and a cutting board (self-healing plastic is excellent) or a sheet of glass (though this will blunt blades very quickly). This stencil is made up of two seemingly unrelated elements, a bold cross and delicate flowers whose bridges are narrow in keeping with the intricacy of the design.

3 The two stencils which make up the teddy design are very much related. One stencil has all the body pieces, separated by narrow 'bridges'. The other has all the details that give the teddy its character. To help in tracing off the correct parts of each stencil onto the separate card pieces, shade in all the details for the second stencil. This one will obviously be stencilled last after the main part of the motif.

The sketch of the rag doll reading her book, drawn from a real doll and not a template, requires a small adaptation before it can be used as a tracing. To add a little realism to the figure, extra head and shoulders need putting back under her hair. This area is marked for clarity with red shading.

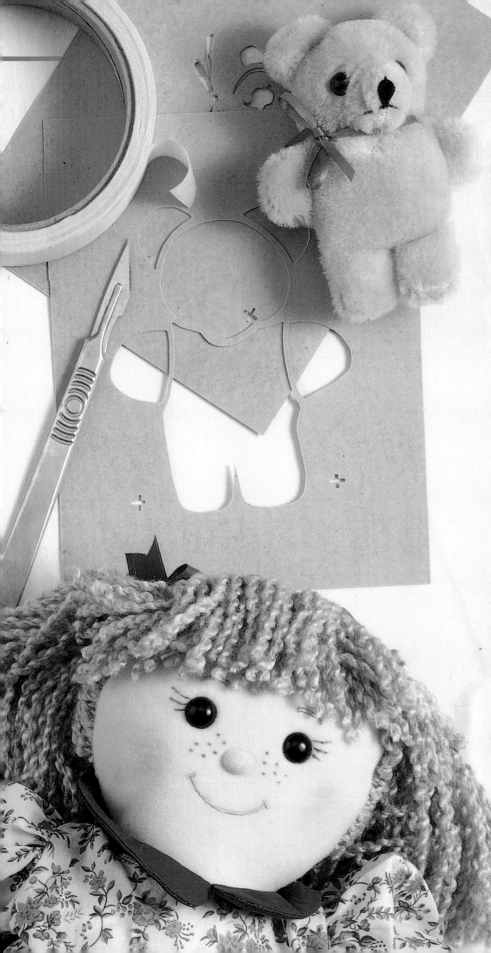

Repairing a stencil

Both stencil card and plastic film are relatively strong, but they can be damaged. In general it is the bridges that snap at one end. Stick broken ends back in place with small pieces of masking tape. Turn over and cut away any excess tape showing. Other vulnerable areas are parts joined at one end only. Re-attach with tape or cut a new piece and stick with tape.

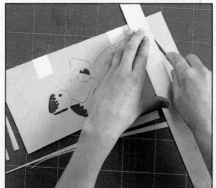

2 Cut all the elements of the stencil. Position carefully over one another and fix together with masking tape on the free side where no form of registration mark is to be made. Place on a cutting board and trim off square. In this case, the doll's 'back' edge was cut close to her body through all layers. Use a steel rule rather than a plastic ruler if you have one.

Registration marks

1 When two or more stencils make up a design, they will require some method of placing one exactly over another. This is done by cutting registration marks through all layers, usually in the form of a cross. When positioning the first element for stencilling, mark the crosses lightly with pencil. Position the second element with its crosses over the marks. Rub off the marks on completion of the project.

3 In certain situations, marking registration crosses is not the best method. In the case of the doll reading her book and leaning up against the door of the dresser, there is limited room for crosses. It is better to cut out notches from her back edge for registration vertically, and to butt the stencil card up to the lower beading for horizontal registration.

Methods of stencilling

The various methods of applying paint all give a different finished result and it is this which determines the method you use. Each method has its advantages and disadvantages, but the brush method is probably the most versatile.

The brush method

1 Use a separate stencil brush for each colour. Decant a little hard-surface paint onto a washable dish. Dip the brush into the colour and dab off the excess onto kitchen paper towel.

2 Apply the paint through the stencil with a dabbing motion, starting at the centre. Dab on other colours to give the effect of shading or use a swirling movement without lifting the brush. The mixure of dabbing and swirling gives a lovely finish on completion. Get to know your brushes as each gives a different texture. This technique adds 'life' to the stencil. It is quick to dry and brushes wash clean in water. It can take time to work and large areas will take longer to cover than if using sponging.

A happy cross between the smoothness of crayons and the marked texture of sponging, stencilling by the brush method is the technique most commonly used.

The sponge method

1 Pour a little of each hard-surface paint required onto a washable dish. Break a natural sponge up into pieces for small areas of stencilling (the holes in man-made sponges are too even in texture). Use a separate, water-dampened sponge for each colour. Dab the sponge with paint and blot off the excess onto kitchen paper towel before applying.

2 The unevenness of the holes in the sponge give a definite texture. If the paint is applied heavily, this starts to disappear. Sponging is quick to cover large areas and the sponges will wash clean in water for re-use. Natural sponge can be expensive, however, and you need to gauge carefully how much paint to blot off first.

The crayon method

1 The oil-based stencil crayon is a relative newcomer to stencilling. It does, however, still need to be applied with a conventional brush. Rub some of the crayon onto a spare piece of card. Using a clean brush for each colour, rub the brush over the colour to lift it off.

2 Apply the paint to the stencil using a large, sweeping circle and starting in the centre and working outwards. Colours can be mixed on the actual stencil as the paint stays wet. Just add one over another and blend in well with the brush. The advantages of crayon are a lovely soft, translucent colour, colours that almost blend themselves and a very quick application time. They do have the disadvantages that they can take several days to dry, the crayons can become very messy and the brushes need cleaning in turpentine.

Notice the smoothness of the painting – the colours merge beautifully into one another with soft edges, and can even be painted to give an almost transparent effect.

The finished result of the sponge method is very textured in feel and is almost spotted in its visual effect. This makes it useful for creating bushes and trees.

Cleaning up:
water-based paint

Masking tape, though wonderful for
providing a straight line to paint against,
always lets a little paint seep under the edge.
As soon as the paint is dry, remove the tape,
pulling it off cautiously. Using clean water
in a container and a clean rag, gently rub
off the unwanted paint. Keep changing to a
clean area of dampened rag.

Cleaning up:
oil-based paint

Here, the oil-based glaze has run
slightly onto the door edges during sponging.
Allow the glaze to dry before handling.
Remove the paint with cotton wool-wrapped
sticks dipped in turpentine, replacing the
stick when dirty. If applying a 'line' of glaze,
remove masking tape when the glaze is touch
dry, cleaning up any excess before the drying
process is finished.

Making piping

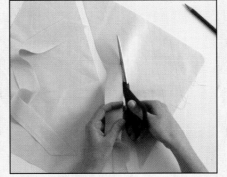

1 Piping cord is available in many widths. Choose one that is appropriate in scale or for the look that you require. Always wash piping cord before use as it shrinks considerably more than the fabric encasing it. A lot of hard work can be ruined otherwise on the first washing. Press fabric to remove any creases. Fold in half diagonally across the grain, that is, at an angle to the selvedges and the weave. This produces lengths of fabric that mould around corners easily. Mark the fold by pressing firmly along it with your fingernail to give a crease.

2 Open out the fabric. With a sharp pencil and ruler, lightly mark lines running parallel to the crease line about 4 cm (1½ in) apart. Using sharp fabric scissors, cut down the crease line made with the fingernail and along the pencil lines to make long strips of fabric for your piping.

3 Place two strips together with right sides facing and raw diagonal ends matching. It should look as though two points are sticking out, one to either side. Pin together and continue to piece the remaining strips together until you have a length long enough for your piping.

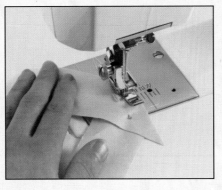

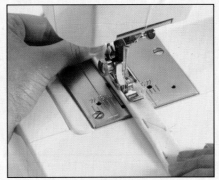

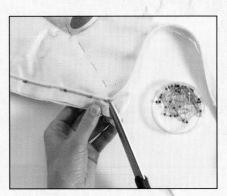

4 Thread up the sewing machine to match the colour of your fabric. Using the piping foot attachment, machine across the ends taking a 1 cm (³/₈ in) seam allowance, and removing the pins as you work. Use the width of the foot attachment as a guide, keeping the inner (right) side running parallel to the raw edge.

5 Trim off the excess fabric close to the stitching lines and press seams open. Lay the piping cord lengthways down the centre of the fabric on the wrong side. Wrap the fabric around the piping and pin in place on the right side. Machine as close to the piping as you can down the entire length of fabric. (The piping foot can be positioned to be right or left-handed.)

6 Starting on the bottom edge, place the piping around the outside edge of cushion front, with raw edges matching. Pin in place along the stitching line. At corners, snip through two layers of piping fabric only up to the stitching line. Where the ends of the piping meet, overlap them neatly. Cut off excess. Machine all around over the previous stitching, taking care at the overlap.

FURNITURE

Preparing, painting
and stencilling furniture is one of the most
rewarding ways of spending a quiet weekend.
If you have ever spent time looking for, but never
finding, that individual design in quite the right colours
then look no further to begin creating your own
custom-made pieces.

ROSE CHEST OF DRAWERS

THIS CHEST OF drawers was in a very sorry state. The old, brown varnish was chipped and scratched and there were a couple of gaping holes on the top and down one side where a backpiece and towel rail had originally been. Luckily all the handles existed and matched as these are difficult and expensive to replace if missing. A carpenter turned a new towel rail, fitting it in the old holes, and plugged the holes on top with circular pieces. It was then ready for its facelift!

1 *Remove the handles. On Victorian chests the handles are usually backed with a turned wooden screw. Simply unscrew the complete handle and screw as one. Rub the varnish off the whole chest, wrapping glasspaper around a sanding or worn-out abrasive block. Wear old clothes and a face mask to protect you from the dust.*

BELOW: *Notice the shading in the stencilling. It adds realism and depth to the flowers and leaves. Try to use three or four pinks in each rose and two greens, plus yellow, brown or white in the foliage.*

2 *Clean any old glue and dirt from the screw part of the handles. Sand off the varnish using a flexible abrasive block, which is easy to rub into the grooves. After sanding, wipe the handles and chest down with a clean rag, dampened in turpentine (see page 102). Paint in off-white eggshell. Stand the handles in bottles or similar to dry.*

4 *Trace and cut out the rose stencils on page 168 using plastic film (see page 106). Stencil the motif using the brush method (see page 108) and three shades of pink and green, two shades of blue, yellow and light brown, and white stencil paints. Use the whole stencil on one half of the lower, largest drawer if possible. To stencil one half of the next drawer, mask the stencil off until you have a design to fit the space available. Repeat for the outer edges of the top drawers. To stencil the other halves of the drawers, turn the stencil over. Clean, wetting kitchen paper towel with cellulose thinners and rubbing carefully over the dried paint. Fill in the middle of the drawers with the small rose and bow designs. Use the smaller elements of the design to decorate the top and frame of the chest, masking off unwanted areas as before.*

3 *The chest and handles will need two coats of off-white eggshell paint. Allow to dry thoroughly between coats and before decorating. Mix a small amount of dull pink glaze in a tiny glass jar (see page 105). Individual jam and marmalade pots are perfect for this purpose. Alternatively, choose a shade that you would like to be dominant in your design. Use a fine artist's brush to decorate the handles with delicate circles painted in the grooves.*

5 *To give the chest an instant antique look, wipe over with furniture wax. This is available in several tints, including 'antique'. Buffing may remove little bits of stencilling but adds to the aged look.*

RIGHT: *Having restored the chest to its former glory, try collecting a few pretty pieces to sit on it that are also antique, a swivel mirror, for instance, or a glass vase for flowers or some crochet-edged linen.*

ORIENTAL WARDROBE

1 *Before stripping or sanding, take an accurate reference of any details in case they become damaged. Take a rubbing with the flat side of a pencil onto tracing paper. Trace the rubbing onto stencil card and cut a stencil (see page 106). Note that it cannot always simply be cut out; bridges must be added at each intersection. Here you would merely cut a circle with knobs.*

2 *To repair missing bits of moulded decoration, use the rubbing made for cutting the stencil. Trace the required area onto a piece of thin cardboard that is the same depth as the moulding (card from food packaging was suitable here). Carefully cut out the replacement piece, trying it for fit and trimming if necessary, and glue in place with all-purpose adhesive.*

N INETEEN-THIRTIES furniture is generally loved or loathed! Much of it is very heavy and cumbersome but some pieces, with a little imagination, can be made into something quite stunning and useful. This single wardrobe first appealed because of the chinese-looking raised decoration on the doors. That instantly suggested an oriental feel – one that was just as popular in the thirties as it still is today.

RIGHT: *Painted and stencilled, a 1930s wardrobe becomes the focal point of the room. To decorate the room in keeping, try pasting oriental-style giftwrap inside wooden moulding on the walls and adding a few fans.*

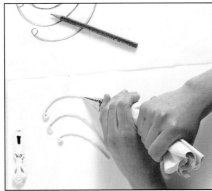

3 *Have large items stripped professionally as this is extremely time consuming by hand. Remove doors and hinges. Leave on any handles to be painted with gesso and with the background colour, making them merge in and disappear. Paint the entire wardrobe and doors with acrylic gesso until the grain of the wood no longer shows. Sand down with fine grade glasspaper between coats. The gesso creates a smooth surface that is reminiscent of chinese lacquer.*

4 *Draw the bird and tree templates on page 169 onto tracing paper. Use the tracings to mark the position of the birds' tail feathers and the tree branches onto the wardrobe surface. Mix up interior plaster filler, spoon into a cake icing bag fitted with a small round nozzle and pipe carefully along the feather and branch lines. Allow to dry.*

ABOVE: This wardrobe had rounded moulding down the doors and edges, just waiting to be painted like bamboo! To copy this look, try gluing and pinning split bamboo cane in place before painting.

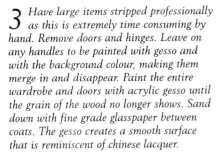

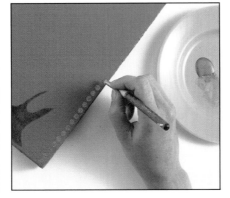

5 *Paint the wardrobe with approximately two coats of matt emulsion in Chinese red. Allow to dry. Pick out the branches of the tree with a little white paint. Use the tracings to cut stencils of the bird body and tree trunks (see page 106) and cut a Chinese circle stencil using the template on page 169 if there are no mouldings present on your wardrobe. Stencil the bird body, the tree trunks and the Chinese circle in gold and black stencil paints, using the brush method (see page 108). Stencil the circle onto the sides of the wardrobe as well as onto the front. To stencil the tree trunks, trim the stencil very close to the cut areas so that it fits in between the plaster branches.*

6 *A moulded beaded edge is often found on 1930s furniture. Copy this in 'stencil' spots. Use the flat end of a small stencil brush dipped in acrylic gold paint to dab dots along the bottom and top edges of the door and wardrobe frame. Pick out any beading, if you have it, in gold using finger-painting. Dip the end of your finger in acrylic gold paint and run gently over the surface to colour. Repeat on any original relief moulding.*

7 *Cut dragonfly stencils using the templates on page 169. Stencil in gold acrylic paint using the brush method and turning the stencil in different directions to create the impression of flying dragonflies. Paint any moulding to imitate bamboo, first painting bands and spots in gold then in black paint, marking in dots and notches. A feature of Chinese lacquer is its smooth, shiny finish. Paint with gloss varnish, checking that the gold paint will not be dulled by it.*

FLORAL CIRCULAR TABLE

1 Fastening catches can be attended to by an antique restorer or replaced at specialist hardware stores. Clean off dirt, any remaining finish and ink stains with a combination of methylated spirits and household bleach. Wearing household gloves, rub on methylated spirits with steel wool and attack any stains with bleach on cotton-covered sticks. Wipe off any residue with a clean rag and then with turpentine. Allow to dry. Repeat if necessary.

2 On the newly stripped wood mark six equal panels. Measure the table top at its widest point from side to side and from top to bottom, marking the centre point in each case. Place the straight edge of a protractor along one marking line with the 90° angle mark along the other. Mark in 60° and 120° angles. Repeat on the other half of the table. Draw in the complete lines from edge to edge, using a long rule.

3 Check the outer motif on page 170 will fit the panels on your table. Reduce or enlarge the template if necessary on a colour photocopier. You will need to cut three stencils for this motif. Trace off onto stencil card all the areas indicated with a black outline and cut out (see page 106). Repeat for the areas outlined with a dotted line for a second stencil, then trace off the remaining areas for the third stencil. Cut a separate stencil using the template on page 170 for the central motif.

THIS ANTIQUE tilt-top table had seen better days, or perhaps was just dearly loved and over-used. The wooden top was badly marked with ink stains – a legacy from writing love letters? One would like to think so. The fastening catch too was well worn and not too reliable at keeping the top in a horizontal position. All in all, it did not seem too wicked giving a Victorian antique piece of furniture a new lease of life with stencilling!

4 Use newspaper to mask off all but one panel. Position the masking tape directly over the drawn lines. In a clean glass jar, make up a glaze, mixing acrylic scumble glaze with a brown tint, both available from specialist paint stores. (Being acrylic, this glaze dries very quickly and the six panels can be treated in quick succession.) Paint onto the panel.

RIGHT: The table in its upright position takes up very little space The decoration is shown off here with the repeating design seen in full. Note how there are no 'bridges'; the leaves and flowers all touch one another.

RIGHT: The marquetry stencil design was inspired by a Regency dining table. The original design would have been brightly coloured but it has now faded to lovely honey shades. It is these pale tones that were copied in the stencilling.

5 *Immediately take up a heartgrainer. Holding the handle, gently rock the grainer across its curved surface while slowly pushing it away from you across the width of the panel, creating woodgraining as you go. Treat the whole panel. This wonderful tool is available in various sizes, to give grain lines from fine to bold. A medium one is used here.*

6 *When dry, remove the paper and mask off the next panel. Repeat the process until all panels are grained. Allow the final panel to dry. With a 3 mm (¹/₈ in) gap between, run two lengths of masking tape through the centre point and across the entire top on either side of the panel edges. Paint in cream acrylic to resemble ivory inlay. Dry and repeat twice, giving divisions between all panels. Finally stencil, registering the outer motif stencils as shown on page 107. Use the brush method (see page 108) and hard surface stencil paints in forest green, lemon, yellow, brown and fawn. Finish by stencilling the central motif.*

TARTAN
DINING CHAIRS

1 *There seemed to be two varnishes on these chairs. A heavy, thick sort on the flat backs and the fine version that can be effortlessly sanded off on the legs. Test parts of a piece of furniture with glasspaper first to see how easy it is to clean before trying paint stripper (see page 102). These chairs required several treatments of stripper to remove the finish.*

W HEN BOUGHT originally, there was only one of these chairs available, then amazingly a few weeks later an identical one was spotted. If possible, never split a pair of items – two not only look better, they are more valuable. The French bistro appearance of these chairs called for a simple but bold approach to the stencilling. A strongly patterned tartan that could be echoed in fabric and accessories seemed the most appropriate solution.

2 *Do not be put off buying chairs with rush seats that are covered with a grey fur. This mould is simply removed by wiping off with a dry cloth or a paper towel. Clean the entire seat with a cloth wrung out in water and detergent. Do not soak it and dry as quickly as possible. The spore causing the mould is in the air all year and lands when rush is wet.*

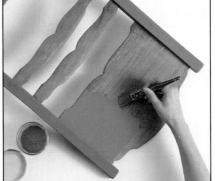

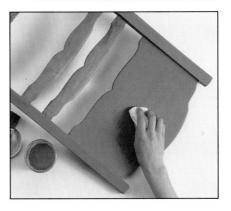

3 An economical way to colour wood after preparing it is with matt emulsion paint. Match the colour with that of the room's colour scheme, or choose an unusual shade like purple. This method works like purchased wood-stains, soaking quickly into the surface but showing the grain through. In a glass jar, dilute the emulsion 50:50 with water. Do not paint the whole chair at once.

4 Depending on the weather and humidity, leave for between a few seconds and ten minutes before wiping off excess paint with a clean cloth. On a hot summer's day or when it is bright and windy, only a few seconds can elapse before the paint is too dry to wipe away. Conversely, in cold, damp or very humid conditions, leave for up to ten minutes.

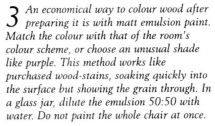

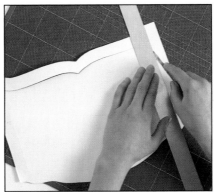

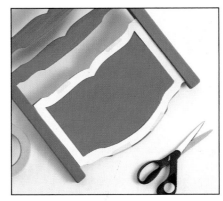

5 Cut a piece of tracing paper the width of the chair back from side to side. Lay the chair on its back, placing the tracing paper on the back-piece. With a pencil, mark the outline edge of the chair back onto the tracing. Cut out along the pencil marks. Place this template on thick paper and cut out. Mark a line 1.5 cm (⅝ in) in from the outer edge. Carefully cut away the centre.

LEFT: Take co-ordination to its limits – why not stencil the skirting boards to match the chair backs? Not the easiest of positions to stencil in – but the result is great fun!

6 Position the paper outline on the chair back with masking tape. Use the template on page 170 to cut three stencils (see page 106) on oblongs of card so the tartan design has straight edges. Position the stencils centrally over the chair to work. Using the brush method (see page 108) and hard surface stencil paints, stencil the lime green check first, then the lemon, then finally the red stripes. The template underneath creates a neat border outline.

HEART
CUPBOARD

ALTHOUGH SMALL, this cupboard had many surfaces to adorn. It is made from solid oak and even before stripping off layers and layers of paint, the very textured grain of the oak was visible. Liming, an old treatment on wood, looks wonderful on the deep grain of oak and is brought up to date here with the addition of colour. The cut-out hearts in the back board became the inspiration for the stencilling.

1 Traditionally, liming was always white and was applied to woods like oak as a preservative to give a long-lasting wood an even greater life span. Liming wax can still be applied in white, though it is now fashionable to tint it. Place some of the wax in a glass bowl and add a teaspoon or two of powder colour in ultramarine. Mix well to the desired shade.

2 Paint the whole cupboard with a coat of matt emulsion in a slightly paler blue than the liming wax. The coloured wax will always be soft in colour because of the whiteness of the wax. When the emulsion is dry, rub the coloured wax onto the parts of the cupboard that are not to be stencilled. Apply it with fine steel wool, wearing rubber gloves if desired.

3 Rub the wax well into the grain of the wood. Leave for about five minutes to dry. Then, using a clean piece of rag, rub off any excess wax from the surface of the wood. The wax in the grain will remain there to emphasise the texture and give a hint of colour.

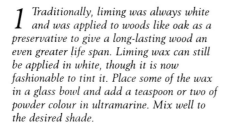

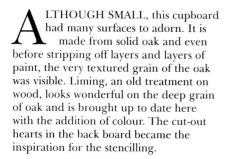

4 To set the wax in the grain and give a protective coating to the colour, rub the waxed areas with a neutral wax furniture polish. Rub it in well with a clean cloth. This will remove a little of the colour but will buff up to a soft sheen with another clean rag. Due to the waxy surface, it is not possible to stencil on limed areas.

5 Use the same soft blues and an apricot in emulsion paint to paint bands of colour along the flat edges of the cupboard. Employ a square-ended brush – its width determines the breadth of the band. When the decoration is dry, cut the stencils (see page 106), using the heart on a ribbon and heart grid templates on page 171. Stencil

with a brush (see page 108), using the illustration as a guide. Use green paint in addition to those mentioned above. The emulsion surface will wear with use, adding to the simple appeal of the cupboard.

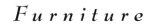

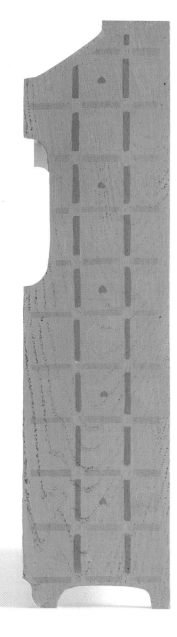

ABOVE: The grain of the wood is visible here, even without liming. The cupboard is painted a soft shade of blue, taken from the Shaker palette and decorated with a simple stencil that imitates the Shaker style.

LEFT: Cupboards such as the one decorated here are a common find in antique fairs and flea markets. They make charming accessories for the house and provide useful storage space in kitchens and bathrooms.

123

ART NOUVEAU FIREPLACE

I F YOU ARE fortunate enough to own a fireplace surround, it might be a little on the plain side and in need of decoration. Alternatively, it is possible to fit a new fireplace surround on an outside wall or into an existing chimney breast. Fireplaces do not have to be working to look good. Painting on a stencilled motif with the addition of an arrangement of dried flowers can create a stunning focal point in a room.

RIGHT: *Follow the marbling instructions on page 103 to create a marble effect for the mantelpiece. Use the honey glaze from the fire surround and make up a dark grey glaze from artist's oil paint and turpentine. Mix two beige/brown glazes for the sponging, referring to the instructions on page 105.*

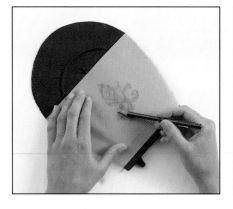

1 It is good design practice to take an existing decorative element present in one section of an .object and to add it to another section in order to give some co-ordination. Here, a rubbing of the raised design on the hood flap was made with the flat side of a pencil onto tracing paper. The tracing was used to cut a stencil for the wooden surround. If you prefer, use the templates on page 171 to cut stencils (see page 106). of the art nouveau motifs that were used to decorate this plain surround, reducing or enlarging the motifs on a photocopier to fit.

2 This fireplace was bought for a song at an outdoor antique market because there was a crack in the hood, meaning it can never be used with a real fire. The thick rust was removed by professional sand-blasters, who immediately painted it with green oxide paint to prevent rust re-forming. The whole of the front metal surface was then painted with black iron paste, available from fireplace stores.

3 Rub the blacked grate vigorously with clean rags to create a soft, burnished look. Re-do this periodically as the sheen will fade over time.

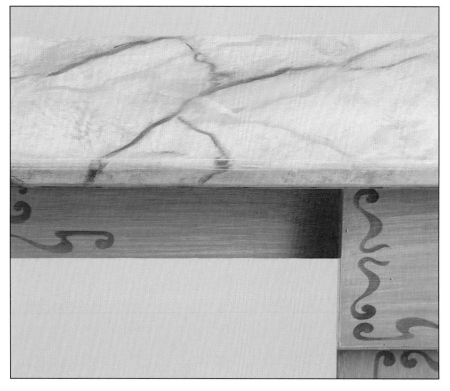

4 The wooden fireplace surround and mantelpiece were made by a local carpenter, who was instructed to make it very simple with as many flat surfaces as possible since these are ideal to stencil. Surrounds can also be bought cheaply from household auctions and flea markets. Paint with several coats of cream eggshell (this also acts as an undercoat). When dry, mix up a honey-coloured glaze (see page 105) and paint on the flat surfaces.

5 Using a very long-haired brush or a specially designed dragging brush, drag the wet glaze. Pull the brush through the glaze, keeping as much area of bristle flat on the glaze as possible. Wipe the excess glaze off the brush with a cloth dampened with turpentine. Do some of the dragging horizontally and some vertically. Clean up stray glaze from the edges of the surround with a cloth dampened in turpentine. Take care not to let the cloth catch on the dragged areas of painting.

6 Stencil, using several shades of green and red oil-based crayons for a soft look (see page 109). Use the colours separately or blended together to create new, differing shades. The surround will need to be left for several days to dry. Varnish if desired.

LEFT: *Allow the stencilling to dry for two or three days before attempting to marble the mantelpiece or fix the surround in place. For non-working fireplaces, carpet can be laid right inside the fire for neatness.*

SEASIDE LINEN BASKET

W ITH MORE AND more interest developing in conservation and doing things up, a great many old and odd bits of furniture are being brought out of retirement to give them a further life span. Objects made in this Lloyd Loom-type of weave are suddenly flooding the market. Some pieces are quite ordinary, but others like this linen basket catch the eye because of their wonderful 1930s shape and, of course, because of their practicality and usefulness.

RIGHT: The introduction of metallic paint for this project hints at the silvery sparkle sunlight makes on the sea and the flash of swimming fish. Emphasize the seaside and watery feel of the sponging on the basket with a flight of scallop shells glued to the wall 1930s style. A hot glue gun is invaluable here.

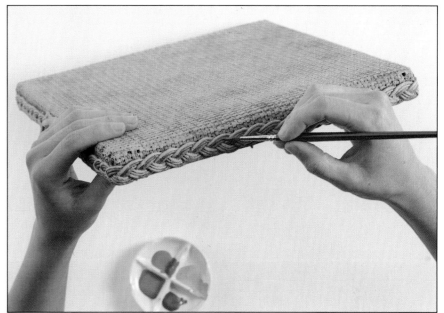

1 As the basket had been heavily re-painted in the past, it was sent to a professional stripper for cleaning up. Their process 'wets' the object less than doing it by hand and it is the damp that ruckles the weave. Remove the lid. Clean any rust and remaining paint off the handles with metal and chrome polish (available from car accessory stores), rubbed on with a clean cloth.

2 This weave has a disadvantage. Over years of repainting, the holes become clogged. Never paint this or Lloyd Loom by hand, always spray paint it with car spray paints or aerosol cans. The weave will be very absorbent for the first few coats. Make up a glaze from dark blue oil-based paint and turpentine (see page 105), sponging randomly to create an underwater effect.

3 Make the most of a woven edge to the lid and basket sides by picking out the individual strands in bright blue, green and metallic red acrylic paints. This is quite painstaking, but well worth the effort. Follow one strand all around in one colour, using a medium-sized artist's brush.

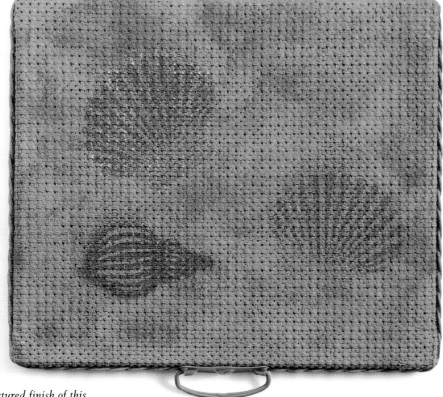

ABOVE: The very textured finish of this woven surface softens the edges of the stencilling, making it merge into the background as though it were underwater.

4 Because of the very textured surface, a stencil will not lie perfectly flat on it. It is therefore essential to use stencils with very little detail and with bold and strong shapes. Use the templates on page 172 to cut a sea urchin and two shell stencils (see page 106). Spray the back of the stencil with spray adhesive well, before positioning on the basket. Make a mask from paper to protect the surrounding area. Spray using metallic car paints in blue, green and red.

FABRIC

It is so easy to design and print your own fabrics using stencils. Fabric paint is simple to use and may be washed with care. Decorate anything from a small cushion to entire curtains to give your home an ornate finish, and delight your children by stencilling their favourite character or animal.

NOAH'S ARK
COT QUILT

EVERYONE SEEMS to delight in making things for children. Perhaps it is just to see that look of enchantment on their faces, especially if the object depicts some of their best-loved characters or stories. This Noah's Ark quilt is bound to find a safe haven on a child's bed. Try making it into a wallhanging and a pile of cushions or stencil a border of marching animals around the room, ending at the ark.

ABOVE: To stencil the second squirrel in reverse, clean the used stencil with cellulose thinners and turn the stencil over.

ABOVE: The giraffe is positioned slightly off-centre in the fabric square. Notice the shading of the markings stencilled on it.

1 The tied bows at the bottom of the quilt are for decoration only. Cut six 40 x 6 cm (15½ x 2¼ in) pieces of check fabric in a contrasting colour to the quilt. Fold in half down their length and pin. Machine along one short end and down the length, taking a 1 cm (⅜ in) seam. Turn through to the right side and press well. Put to one side.

3 Lay the squares out in order with right sides up. Machine-sew into horizontal sets of three, taking 1 cm (⅜ in) turnings and with right sides facing. Now sew the five horizontal sets together along their top and bottom edges, taking the same seam allowance as before and with right sides facing. Press the seams open on the reverse side and set the paint according to the manufacturer's instructions.

2 From plain cotton fabric, cut eight blue and seven white squares, all measuring 22 cm (8½ in) square. Cut stencils, using the templates on pages 172–173, from 20 cm (8 in) squares of card (see page 106). Tape the squares of fabric firmly to a flat surface – kitchen worktops are ideal. Using the illustration as a guide, stencil the animal motifs in appropriate colours – yellow, brown, beige and grey. Stencil the waves, the ark, Noah and his wife in shades of blue, adding red to the ark. Use the brush method (see page 108) and keep the stencils in place with spray adhesive. Note that the giraffe, and Noah and his wife are not centred on the square.

4 For the border, cut two pieces of large-checked blue gingham 102 x 24 cm (40 x 9½ in) for the sides and two pieces 106 x 24 cm (42 x 9½ in) for the top and bottom. Machine sew the side borders in place taking 1 cm (⅜ in) seams and having right sides facing. Add the top and bottom pieces, right sides facing, joining them to the squares and the side borders and taking 1 cm (⅜ in) seams. Press all seams open.

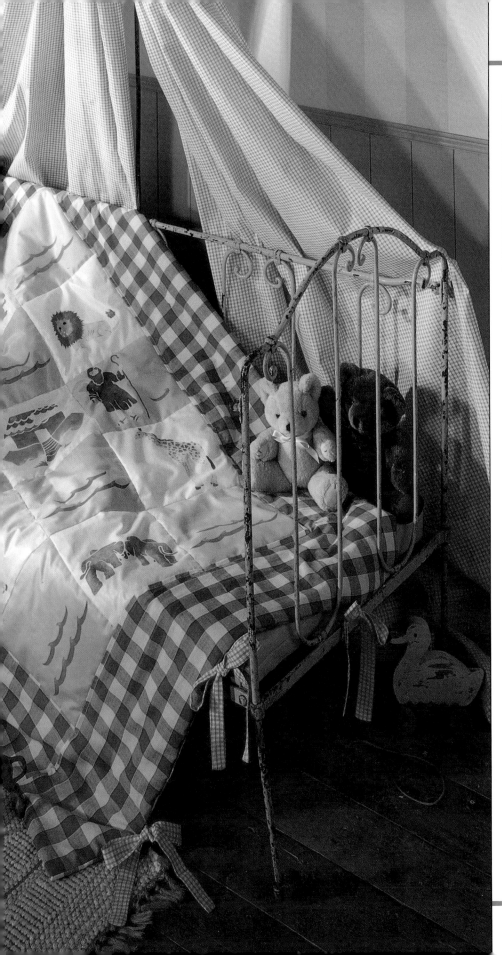

5 *From large-checked blue gingham fabric, cut a piece for the back measuring 106 x 146 cm (42 x 57½ in), joining lengths if necessary. Cut a similar sized piece from light-weight polyester wadding for the padding. Lay the back piece out with the right side up. Over it, place the front piece with the wrong side up and cover both with the wadding.*

6 *Pin the three layers (top, back and wadding) together around the top and side edges, taking a generous seam allowance of 3 cm (1⅛ in) and leaving a gap of 76 cm (30 in) at the bottom. Trim off the excess to 1 cm (⅜ in) and cut off all corners close to the stitching line. Turn the quilt right side out. Trim wadding along the open edge, and turn in 3 cm (1⅛ in) to the inside at the front and back, tucking in the three pairs of ties at regular intervals. Sew the gap closed.*

LEFT: The finished quilt should be laundered carefully in hand-wash detergent. The French metal bed on which the quilt is displayed in this picture is a photographer's prop only and is not recommended for a young child to sleep in.

7 *Lay the quilt out flat and run large basting stitches from side to side and from top to bottom to hold the layers together firmly. Machine up and down in the seams where the stencilled squares join and similarly from side to side. Finish the machine quilting by running a line of stitching around the border, 1 cm (⅜ in) from the edge of the squares. Remove the basting and make the ties into bows. Add some quilting knots to the border. Using double thread, take a stitch through all layers on the right side, leaving the loose ends long. Take a back stitch, bringing the needle out in the same place. Remove the needle, tie the loose ends into a knot and trim. Make six on each side and four each at the top and bottom.*

NURSERY CUSHIONS

TEDDIES AND rabbits are amongst the most popular of motifs for children of all ages. Here, they have been stencilled on cushions to decorate the nursery, although a little fabric ted found his way into the picture along with a tiny cupboard! Should you have a favourite teddy or toy in the house, try designing your own stencil to create a very personal and special nursery or child's bedroom (see page 106). Otherwise, use the templates on page 174 to cut stencils from plastic film.

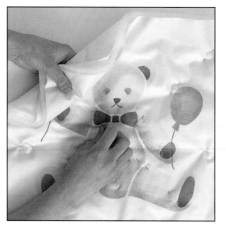

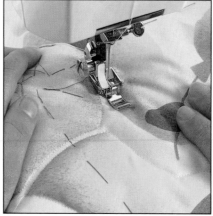

1 Wash and dry your fabric. Cut squares, circles or rectangles of fabric large enough to accommodate the chosen motif with a 1 cm (⅜ in) seam allowance added. Choose appropriate coloured fabric stencil paints and stencil the motifs onto the fabric, keeping the fabric taped down flat. Use the brush method (see page 108), keeping the stencil film in place with spray adhesive. Employ shading to add life and form to the teddies and rabbits, using a darker shade than the basic body colour. For a quilted cushion cover, place the stencilled fabric right side up over light-weight wadding and muslin. Pin and baste the three layers together with large stitches, starting at the centre each time and sewing to each corner and to the middle of each side.

2 Thread the sewing machine with cotton to match the stencil colouring. Fit the piping foot – this gives a good edge to run along the perimeter of the motif because the needle follows along the edge of the foot. Machine all around the motifs, picking out details for sewing around as well. Pull the ends through to the wrong side with a sewing needle and secure.

3 Make piping as described on page 111. Pin in place around the edges of the right side of the stencilled square, raw edges matching. Tack over pinning and machine in place. Remove the tacking, cut and lay the fabric back on top of the cushion front with right sides facing. Pin in place. Machine over previous stitching on three sides. Trim off excess fabric close to the piping, clip the corners and turn through to the right side. Insert a cushion pad and sew up the opening.

4 To make a nine-panelled cushion requires accuracy. Use a set square to ensure that corners are a true 90°. Mark the cutting line lightly with a pencil right across the fabric, then sub-divide this into 15 cm (6 in)squares. Stencil each square and join them down side seams in sets of three. Finally, sew three rows together. Pipe and finish (see page 111) as for step 3.

5 For the walking teddy cushion, cut two stencils from clear plastic film (its transparency helps placement of the repeating pattern), using the template on page 174. Find the fabric centre by folding in half and centre the teddy 'body' on the fold. Stencil the body first using the brush method and fabric paints in honey and brown for shading. Then use the second stencil to fill in the details in brown paint, adding a red scarf. Stencil two more teddies to either side, marking the position of the previous teddy in permanent marker pen on the edges of the body stencil to help place the stencil correctly each time. Make up the cushion as for step 3.

LEFT: *Mix images of various sizes to create interest and make objects from stencilled fabric that need occasional washing only (launder carefully in hand-wash detergent). Continue the nursery theme by stencilling other objects in the room. Here the teddies come to life marching across a pretty wall cupboard. Stencil them onto stripped and sanded wood (see page 102) and protect with furniture wax, buffed to a soft shine.*

Fabric

EGYPTIAN
BATHROOM

THE BATHROOM is an often neglected room in the house. A sad thought when you consider how much time is spent in there relaxing in a hot bath. It takes very little time to create a peaceful haven – try stencilling on a plain blind or make a fabric shower curtain to hang decoratively outside the plastic waterproof variety. Even tiles can be stencilled successfully with a little help from a can of special varnish!

1 To echo the crenellated edge of the blind illustrated, find the centre and mark lightly with a pencil, then measure out to either side. Calculate the lengths of tape needed to form a channel 2.5 cm (1 in) wide with three evenly spaced crenellations. Run 2.5 cm (1 in) wide masking tape out onto a cutting board, and use its grid lines to cut the tape squarely and accurately. Stick two lines of tape onto the blind forming the channel. Mix up a blue glaze (see page 105), paint and rag roll the area between the tape (see step 4 of the Classic Rug on page 137).

BELOW: *The blue, rag-rolled crenellation represents the Nile, which has plants growing on its banks and water containers waiting to be filled. The sphinxes are instantly recognizable while the flowers are a traditional ancient Egyptian motif.*

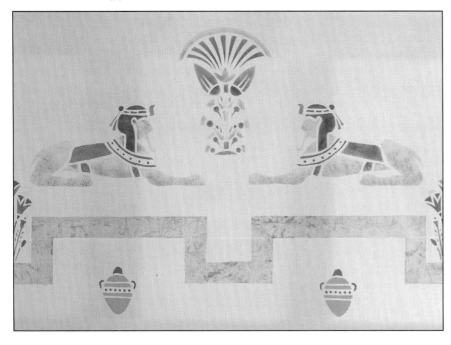

RIGHT: *On a large area like the shower curtain, spread the motifs out well or you will be there all day stencilling! Do not pay too much attention to the top area of the blind either – most of the time it's rolled up.*

2 Cut palm tree, water carrier, flower and sphinx stencils (see page 106) using the templates on page 175. Work the design on the blind, using hard surface paints and the brush method (see page 108). Use strong shades of red, green, blue and yellow. Complete one half before reversing the stencils for other half. To clean the stencil before turning over, wet kitchen paper towel with cellulose thinners and carefully rub over the paint to dissolve it. Work in a well-ventilated room – the fumes can be unpleasant if inhaled.

3 To calculate the fabric required for the curtain, measure the height of the finished curtain and add 16 cm (6½ in) for turnings. Join widths if necessary. Turn in the selvedges to the wrong side and machine-sew. Along the top, turn down a double 4 cm (1½ in) hem and machine close to the fold. Repeat on the bottom. Count up the number of top rings needed and mark on the curtain top. Working on an old piece of wood with a small hammer, make eyelet holes with a purchased eyelet set. Stencil the curtain with fabric paints to match the blind, using the illustration as a guide.

4 Tiles must be dry and free from any traces of grease or dust before stencilling. Wash down with sugar soap and dry well. Stencil using the brush method (see page 108) and use paints in bright colours that are reminiscent of Egyptian designs. To colour in little areas of the stencil, it may be easier to abandon the stencil brush in favour of a stiff artist's brush.

5 Notice that the stencil does not have to be directly centred over the tile – some flowers have been positioned as though growing out of the base of the tile, as they are along the crenellated border on the blind. Protect your hard work with a coat of ceramic varnish, painting over the entire area of the tile.

135

Fabric

CLASSIC RUG

IN TERMS OF decorating, the floor is generally forgotten or the last to be considered. Yet here is a huge expanse to be played with. Floor rugs are not only functional but decorative too. They look best set against plain floorboards, where the eye is naturally drawn to them. Apart from providing visual interest, they also help to insulate and keep a room warm by blocking out cold and draughts.

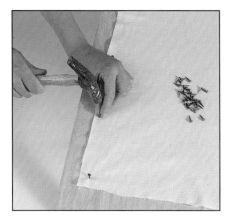

1 This rug measures 70 x 136 cm (27½ x 53½ in). You will need a piece of heavy artist's canvas at least 20 cm (8 in) larger all around than the finished size. Press the canvas, then pin to a large sheet of board with upholstery tacks and a hammer. Start by tacking down at the middle of each side and work out towards the corners – do not hammer the tacks in fully.

RIGHT: *The simplicity of a classical design is hard to beat. The subtle colouring and geometry of the pattern fits in with most styles of decoration and blends well with furniture of all ages.*

2 Paint the entire area of the canvas with white acrylic primer, diluted 50:50 with water. Paint lightly, trying not to work the paint in too hard – you do not want it coming through on the other side of the fabric if possible. Apply three or four undiluted coats, letting each one dry before applying the next.

3 Pull out the tacks and trim the edges off square using a steel rule, set square and sharp craft knife. Mark a line 2.5 cm (1 in) all around the edge and another, 5 cm (2½ in) inside that. Carefully trim off each corner close to the inner marked line. Turn cloth over to the wrong side. Fold in a hem along the first marked line and then along the second. Stick hems with PVA glue. Allow to dry. Sand smooth any cracks and paint the back with one coat of primer.

4 On the right side, lightly mark a line 8 cm (3 in) in from the edge all around and another 15 cm (6 in) inside that. Run masking tape on either side of these lines, making good, square corners. Mix up a pale green glaze (see page 105). Paint it between the lines of the tape. Immediately dampen a clean rag with turpentine, roll up and run over the glaze to partially remove it. Run tape around the outside edge and paint and rag roll between this and the previous tape. Also rag roll the central area with grey glaze. When dry, cut stencils of the two motifs from the templates on page 176 (see page 106) and stencil with a brush (see page 108) in shades of green, dark brown and tan, using hard surface paints. Seal with acrylic floor varnish.

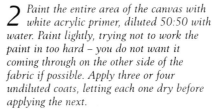

SEA CREATURES
DECK CHAIR

E VEN THE MOST hard-working of us need to relax sometime. Whether it is lazing on a sunny beach or out in the back garden, a comfortable, padded chair is essential. A coat of glistening new paint and newly-stencilled covers will transform a dingy old deck chair. If you are lucky, you may find a deck chair complete with footrest for putting your feet up as well – add a head pillow too and you will never go back to work!

1 Lay the chair and the footrest, if you have one, out flat, taking care not to catch your fingers in the frame. Carefully ease out the old tacks holding the fabric in place and keeping the old canvas as reference for sizing later. Remove the metal hooks from the footrest, storing them safely.

2 Remove any paint finish from the wood, following the directions on page 102. Sand down the wood and the metal hooks with glasspaper or steel wool until smooth. Purchase two cans of spray paint suitable for both wood and metal. These paints need no undercoating and dry quickly. If possible, hang the frame from an 'S' hook while painting it. Spray paint the wooden frames all over. If you have them, spray paint the footrest metal hooks. Wear a protective face mask to help prevent inhaling the vapour.

3 Deckchair canvas is produced to fit the frames and has a selvedge down each side. However, the footrest is usually slightly narrower than the chair and turnings must be taken. Use the old canvas pieces as a measurement for the new fabric length, cutting two pieces for the chair. Cut sea monster and fish stencils using the templates on page 177 (see page 106) and stencil one deckchair piece and the footrest with fabric stencil paints in red and green with yellow for the fish eyes, plus acrylic silver. Attach the canvas to the frame with 13 mm (½ in) bronzed upholsterer's nails and a magnetic-headed hammer.

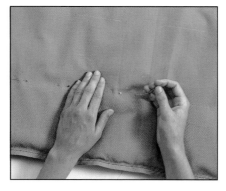

4 Press the deckchair pieces if necessary and lay the stencilled piece the wrong side up and cover with the second piece. Pin down either side and machine together with buttonhole thread 1 cm (⅜ in) from the edge. Cut heavy-weight wadding 20 cm (8 in) shorter than the canvas and insert between the two pieces of fabric with an even border at each end. Run two lines of basting, evenly spaced, down the length. Machine along these lines. Attach to the deck chair frame as for the footrest.

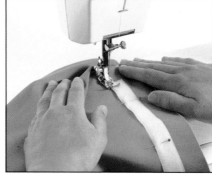

5 For the head pillow, cut two pieces of canvas 41 x 36 cm (16 x 14 in). Stencil one piece as before. Press to set the paint. Lay right side up with the second piece on top. Sew the sides and bottom edges, taking 1 cm (⅜ in) seams. Cut a piece of wadding that fits the width but that is 10 cm (4 in) shorter in depth. Cut a 36 cm (14 in) length of stick and sew, hook and loop fastener. Stick one half to the back of the chair frame and sew the other half to the top edge of the pillow back. Turn the pillow to the right side and insert the wadding. Turn in raw edges and slip stitch closed.

RIGHT: For an individual look on the beach, decorate bright, new canvas with fantastic sea monsters in lurid red and silver. Paint the wooden frame to match for a stunning co-ordinated look.

FRILLED SEAT COVERS

1 *Make a pattern of the missing seat from a sheet of newspaper. Tape the paper on firmly so that it does not slip. Using a steel rule and marker pen, gently feel for the inside edge of the seat and mark a line about 1 cm (⅜ in) outside this around the front and sides. Mark the curved back edge freehand. Cut around the marked lines with paper scissors.*

CLASSIC KITCHEN and dining room chairs like these dainty oak ones are easy to pick up cheaply, especially if, like these, the seats were missing. Originally the seats had been caned but this is expensive and time consuming to have re-done or try doing yourself. Although the loose weave of the caned finish is in keeping with the style of the chairs, adding pretty, frilled seat covers creates the same lightness of feel.

2 *Oak has a marked open grain which takes colouring or liming beautifully. Open the grain further with a large wire brush, rubbing firmly in the direction of the grain. Work out of doors if possible or wear a face mask as the dust produced is very fine. Work into the corners with a shoe suede brush. This should remove all traces of the original finish or varnish.*

3 *Brush off any dust left from the wirebrushing and rub over the chairs with a clean rag dampened in turpentine. Stain with purchased coloured wood dye in apple green, following the directions in step 4 on page 121. Use the paper seat pattern to cut new seat boards from 5 mm (⅕ in) thick plywood, using an electric jigsaw or cutting by hand with a fretsaw. Sand the edges smooth with glasspaper and position over the chair. Hold in place with 13 mm (½ in) bronzed upholsterer's nails. Start in the centre of each side and work into the corners.*

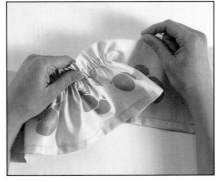

4 From 120 cm (48 in) wide cream fabric, cut two 13 cm (5 in) deep pieces the width of the fabric for the frill. Sew together down one short edge, right sides facing. Cut cabbage, tomato, carrot and bean stencils (see page 106) using the templates on page 178. Use a brush (see page 108) to stencil the right side of the frill with tomatoes, using fabric stencil paints in red, green and white. On the bottom edge, turn up a double 1.5 cm (½ in) hem and machine sew. On the top edge, machine sew double lines of long stitches, breaking off and starting again every 60 cm (24 in). Pull up the stitching to gather.

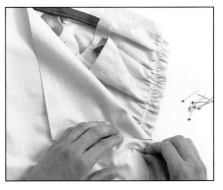

5 Make a pattern of the seat, adding a 1 cm (⅜ in) seam all around. Cut two seat pieces from cream fabric. Stencil one with vegetables. Make 150 cm (59 in) of contrast piping (see page 111) in burnt orange and sew all around the stencilled front piece. Cover the piping on the sides and front edge with the gathered frill, matching raw edges. Machine in place. Place the back piece over the front with right sides facing and with the frill tucked inside. Machine in place leaving the back edge open.

6 Trim away the excess fabric around the sides and front edges. Clip at the corners right up to the stitching line and around any curves. Cut medium-weight wadding to fit inside the seat. Turn the seat to the right side and press well, setting the paint following the manufacturer's instructions. Slip the wadding inside.

7 Cut four 60 x 20 cm (24 x 8 in) pieces of cream fabric for ties. Fold in half down the length of each one and machine along one short edge and along the long edge, tapering the stitching away from the raw edge to form a narrow open end measuring 5 cm (2 in). Trim away excess fabric and turn to the right side. Pin and machine the narrow ends of two ties over the piping in both corners of the open back edge. Machine over previous stitching. Turn in the raw edges of the seat and slip stitch closed. Place on the chair, tying bows around the back struts.

DECORATIVE EFFECTS

Use stencils to play decorative tricks on walls, floors and furniture. Mosaics, tiles, frosted and patterned glass can all be imitated to stunning effects while *trompe l'oeil* shelves, windows and garden screens will delight and amuse your friends.

GEOMETRIC PATIO & POTS

CONSERVATORY or patio paving and containers are often left undecorated, but they cry out to be painted with stencils to elevate them from the humble and hum-drum. Take the classical theme even further by stencilling the walls with the mosiac motif and concealing garden statuary among your plants. Decorate planters and containers in complementary style with bold geometric lines, inventing your own designs to add a personal creative touch.

RIGHT: Old or tired-looking tiles can be given a new lease of life with a simple stencil. The mosaic motif illustrated here is reminiscent of Roman decoration and is ideally suited to a conservatory. Leave the main thoroughfare undecorated as the paint will wear off very quickly or give the floor several coats of varnish to protect it. For speed, three basic colours were used with no shading so that kneeling was kept to a minimum.

MOSAIC TILES

1 Using the templates on page 186, cut stencils from clear plastic film (see page 106) for the border and corner squares. Trace and cut out the central green squares for both border and corners on a separate sheet of film. Using a stencil brush (see page 108) and red and black hard-surface stencil paints, stencil a border of red and black squares. Use the transparency of the film to position it over the matching end of the length you have just painted in order to keep your border straight. Position the centre 'green' stencil between them and stencil in green. Stencil each corner, using the illustration as a guide for positioning and painting the black and red squares first. Mask off the colour not being painted to avoid mistakes. Position the central squares and stencil in green.

2 Using the stencil on page 186 cut a quarter circle stencil from a square of clear plastic film (see page 106). This should fit tiles 29 cm (11½ in) square but it can be reduced or enlarged on a photocopier to fit your own tiles. Align the edges of the stencil with those of the tile and stencil in red and black, masking off the colour not being used as before.

RIGHT: *Plain watering cans and pots may be fine for the garden, but in a conservatory they can be livened up with strong geometric stencil designs that complement the classical mosaic tiles.*

ALUMINIUM POT

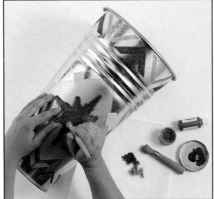

1 When stencilling around curved objects, simple shapes and designs made up from several repeating elements work best of all. Again, using the stencil on page 186, cut star and border designs from clear plastic film (see page 106). On metallic curved surfaces such as this, it is necessary to tape the stencil film down extra firmly. Spray adhesive may also be necessary on the reverse of the stencil. Hold down the points of the stars if necessary. Stencil the star motif using a brush (see page 108) and red hard-surface paints. Stencil the triangular border motifs using red and gold paints. Decorate any raised bands on the pot with lines of green paint.

WATERING CAN

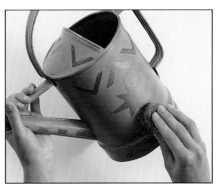

1 Use glasspaper to sand the watering can smooth. Remove any rust and paint with red oxide primer. Paint in a top coat of green eggshell. When dry, use the same stencils and paints as for the aluminium pot and stencil in red and gold to match. Add a gold 'lining' around any raised rims, using gold acrylic paint and a medium-sized artist's brush. Hold the can steady while you work. As the paintbrush is run along, a finger of the same hand runs parallel along the rim, acting as a measure and a steadier.

2 To give the watering can a fashionable antique feel, rub off some of the decoration and the top coat with fine grade steel wool. Concentrate on areas that would rub off naturally, like the handle and sides.

FRENCH BREAD BIN

1 *After stripping the bin back to the bare wood (see page 102), check for any signs of woodworm in the form of little holes, as though made by a thumb tack. In the spring, any patches of wood dust are a tell-tale sign of woodworm. Spray well with a proprietary brand of woodworm killer. Flatten a warped lid by laying between damp newspapers under a heavy weight until it has dried. Repeat if necessary.*

WHEN IT COMES to food and design, the French always seem to come up with something unusual and functional. A tall wooden bin to store their long sticks of bread is no exception. Its flat surfaces are very appealing to the stenciller but do require some ingenuity to fill the tall shape. Hence the cat sitting in the window.

ABOVE: Position the stencil carefully, so that the mouse sits in front of the pot, with his tail hanging over the edge of the windowsill. Add individual hairs, whiskers and highlights to eyes with an artist's brush.

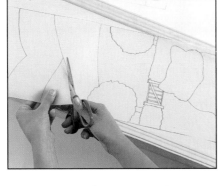

BELOW: *To create the texture of the kitten's fur, use a large, stiff stencil brush – the sort that does not give an even colour and would normally be relegated to the bottom of the box! The natural effect is produced by using lots and lots of different colours – very dark brown, tan, cream and grey shades, some in very small patches only.*

2 *Cover the bin with several layers of eggshell paint in pale cream and allow to dry. To create the background sponged effect, mix an oil-based glaze (see page 105). It looks best as a darker shade of the base colour. Paint the glaze over areas that are not being stencilled. Dampen a natural sponge with turpentine and dab all over the glaze to partially remove it. Clean the sponge regularly with more turpentine.*

3 *Cut a piece of tracing paper the same size as the panel to be stencilled. Using the templates on page 179, draw in a windowsill at the bottom and draw the cat sitting on it to one side. Sketch in the hedge, trees and hills in the background, lengthening or shortening them to fit your bin. Cover with another piece of tracing and draw in the main outlines only. Cut out the different elements carefully with paper scissors.*

4 *Using the original drawing as a guide, place the cut-out templates in position on the front panel and draw around their outside edges with a soft pencil. The raised edge on the front of this bin acted as a natural frame for the stencilled picture. On the sides of the bin, a margin of a few centimetres (1-2 in) was left all around the 'picture', to echo the front raised edge.*

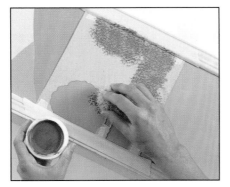

5 *Little pots of emulsion paint are ideal for painting in the background and the garden. Buy two greens and a blue. Mix together a small amount from both pots of green to create another shade and use to paint in the hills and the foreground. Remember, the farthest hill will be the palest. Add sky. The eggshell paint forms the blind background and the sill. Paint the tartan blind with lines of red, using a square-ended artist's brush, and lines of green, using a fine brush. Paint in birds in grey.*

LEFT: *A French bread bin is at home in any kitchen. Pick the base colour to match or tone with your existing units and keep it pale – it will need to be painted over by lots of other shades.*

6 *Cut a stencil for the tree/hedge and gate. Dampen a natural sponge with open holes with water. Thin a little stencil paint in a darker green than the hills. Dip the sponge into the paint and clean off any excess onto kitchen paper towels. Dab lightly through the stencil to form trees and a hedge. Note that the stencil has open edges; mask well here. Stencil the gate and tree trunks in brown hard-surface paints, using the brush method (see page 108).*

7 *'Paint' apples on the trees using a large stencil brush. Dip the bristles into red stencil paint but do not remove the excess paint as usual. Press the brush firmly down to produce a circle or spot. Add highlights in white. Stencil the cat using the template as a reference and paint in the details by hand. Use a fine artist's brush and stencil paints to add whiskers, hair, and highlights to the eyes (see page 102). Continue the hills, hedge, trees and blind on the sides. Cut stencils of the mouse and pot of chives (see pages 106–107). Stencil the pot on each side in terracotta, brown and two shades of green and purple. Stencil the mouse on one side only. Colour him in two shades of brown, with pink ears and nose and black eyes. Add highlights in white to the eyes and additional hairs in brown and white (see page 102).*

CHILD'S DRESSER

DECORATING anything in miniature is always appealing. It is not only the small scale that is fascinating but the memories of childhood that are conjured up too. The previous owner of this child's dresser had started work on restoring it, but sadly had given up halfway through. Panels had been added at the sides to hide some defect and were removed to show a very damaged base, probably due to being stored somewhere damp.

RIGHT: *Pink and blue are the obvious colours for a little girl's dresser, but you can choose a colour scheme to match it with its surroundings. On the back of the shelves stencil books, plates, a seated doll and a ted.*

1 Add interest to the little doors using moulding. Mark the outside edge position of the moulding with a pencil. Carefully measure and cut pieces of moulding to the appropriate lengths, using a 45° mitre block and a fine, sharp saw. Each length is mitred at both ends with the cut angled away from the inside to the outside. Spread the underside of each length with wood glue.

2 Position the glue-backed moulding pieces onto the door, placing the outside edges on the pencil lines. Press down firmly and remove any glue that seeps out with a damp cloth. Pin the moulding in place, using a small hammer and 20 mm (¾ in) panel pins. Fill in any gaps or defects at the mitred corners with fine surface filler using a filler knife.

3 Moisture had started to lift up the top layers of the plywood sides along the bottom edge of this dresser. Cutting a curve at this point not only removed some of the damaged area but also added interest to the plain side. Mark a shallow curve with a pencil and carefully cut along it with a sharp fret saw. Fill where necessary with fine surface filler and sand smooth the entire dresser and the doors with glasspaper.

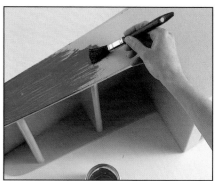

4 Paint the entire dresser with pink eggshell paint and allow to dry. In a wide-mouthed glass jar, mix up a strong coloured glaze (see page 105) made from a touch of white eggshell paint, artist's oil in ultramarine, and turpentine. Paint one side only using a household decorating brush, removing any drips that form on the edges.

5 Immediately, take a rubber comb and run gently but firmly in a straight line from one end to the other. Repeat the process until the whole side has a pattern of lines on it. Clean the excess paint off the comb with a clean rag each time a line of combing is completed. Repeat the process of combing in the opposite direction to form a grid effect. If a mistake occurs, clean the glaze off with turpentine on a rag and repeat.

6 Pick out the moulding, the door handles, the edges of the side pieces and the front edges of the shelves with the same blue glaze. Paint on with care and remove any drips with turpentine on a clean rag. Allow the glaze to almost dry, then wipe over it with a turpentine-dampened rag so that some of the glaze is removed. Comb the outer area outside the moulding on the doors.

LEFT: A dresser is the perfect place for a small girl to store all her treasures, pretty doll's china and little books. The doors were removed for painting and stencilling and were rehung on the original brass and copper hinges which polished up beautifully. New handles were painted to match the blue edging.

7 Use the templates on page 180 to cut a standing and a sitting rag doll stencil, a teddy, a plate, a cup and saucer and a books stencil (see pages 106–107). Stencil the motifs over the shelves and onto the doors, using hard surface paints and the brush method (see page 108). You will need two or three shades of blue, green, red and tan paints, plus black for the rag doll's facial features and shoes. To stencil a rag doll facing in both directions, clean the paint off the used side of the stencil with cellulose thinners in a well-ventilated room, turn over and stencil on the other side. When the stencilling is dry, clean or replace the hinges and handles and rehang the doors.

149

Decorative Effects

FROSTED DOOR PANELS

SADLY, PLAIN featureless doors are common in many houses. Being perfectly flat they are crying out to be stencilled, but a radical facelift before stencilling will transform them even more. Creating panels not only adds character, it restricts the stencilled decoration to a specific area making it visually much stronger. Inserting glass in the top panels adds another dimension, providing a different surface to work on and giving a totally new effect.

RIGHT: Having created a period-style door, look out for an art nouveau finger plate and a large brass knob. Decorate the door frame as though it were made from joined pieces of wood by painting with a deep pink glaze and dragging it.

150

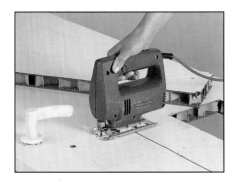

LEFT: *Decorated glass to complement your room decor is easy to achieve. Refer to art books for inspiration for your pattern, whether art nouveau, floral or geometric.*

1 Measure and draw four rectangular panels onto a plain door with a flat surface. Leave the largest widths of frame at the bottom of the door, on a level with the handle, and down the centre. The width at the top of the frame and down either side should be slightly narrower. With a wood bit in an electric drill, make holes in each corner of each panel. Slip the blade of the jigsaw into a hole and carefully cut out each oblong-shaped panel. If you do not have a jigsaw, rent one from a tool hire store, or a carpenter can cut the panels for you.

2 Cut eight pieces of 15 mm (⅝ in) beading to fit each opening – four for the front of the door and four for the back. Tack all the front beading in place, using a hammer and 20 mm (¾ in) panel pins. Make sure the outermost edge of the beading sits level with the front plane of the door. The back beading will fit similarly later.

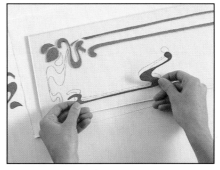

3 Having fitted the front beading, hold the back beading in place to calculate the thickness of glass or plywood needed to fit the gap that is left. If you cannot get an exact fit, the back beading will need to be fitted slightly deeper into the panel opening. Cut plywood pieces for bottom panels and fix in place with the beading and 20 mm (¾ in) panel pins. Sand down paintwork on the door with glasspaper, clean off dust with turpentine on a rag and paint in a pale shade of pink. Paint the entire surface of the door front with a deep pink glaze (see page 105) as quickly as possible. With a dragging brush pull through the glaze, starting and finishing where the joins would be in a period door. With a rag dampened in turpentine, clean glaze from the beading.

4 Stencilling is usually done by applying paint through holes. To create a frosted glass effect, it is the cut-out pieces from the 'holes' that are used. Trace the art nouveau motif template on page 182 onto two pieces of card the same size as your panels. Remember to allow for the depth of the beading around the edge. Lengthen or shorten the design as necessary. Cut out the art nouveau design on both pieces of card with a scalpel or sharp craft knife, making the edges as smooth as possible.

5 Keep the cut-out pieces carefully in a clear plastic folder. Have two glass panels cut to fit by a glazier. Place one over the original tracing of the motif. Trace the design out again on paper as a mirror image of the first. Place the second glass panel over it. Lay them side by side for working. Use spray adhesive to position the back of each cut-out piece on the glass over its counterpart on the drawing below. Press down firmly.

6 Paint the entire surface with clear, polyurethane matt varnish. If possible, use a new can of matt varnish and a clean brush. Any dust that settles on the wet varnish can spoil the finished, frosted effect. Run over the varnish with a clean, fluff-free roller. It will whiten or 'frost' the varnish. When dry, repeat twice more. Alternatively, spray three or four times with satin varnish, allowing it to dry between each application. Remove the cut-outs with great care when the varnish is dry. Clean away any glue with a cotton-wrapped stick dipped in lighter fuel. Fit the glass into the panel openings and fix as for the plywood pieces. Stencil the plywood pieces in pink with a brush (see page 108), using the stencils created when cutting the pieces for frosting.

151

COUNTRY CUPBOARD

IN NATURAL, waxed pine, this wall cupboard looked good in the farmhouse kitchen from where it was bought. But taken out of its old country setting, it needed special treatment to give it back some life. Hence the bright, strong colours and the dramatic crackle finish. The country feel was retained in the simple stencilling on the glass doors.

BELOW: The entire cupboard was painted burgundy inside and out, then the lime green and crackle glazing were added to the top, sides and handles only as a contrast. Varnish with clear, matt polyurethane to add protection.

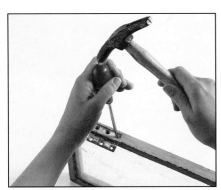

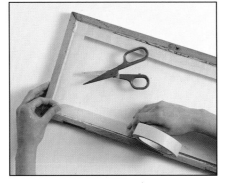

1 Remove the doors and take off the hinges before preparing the wood (see page 102). Keep the hinges and screws safely. Screws on old furniture are often difficult to remove. If the top of the screw is worn flat, try gently hammering the end of the screwdriver, so that its point is forced into the metal for a better grip. Spray with penetrating oil to loosen if all else fails.

2 Strip off any old wax finish with methylated spirits and medium grade steel wool. Place the cupboard or door on plenty of newspaper while doing this to absorb the dirty methylated spirits. Clean the glass. Mask both sides of the glass ready for painting.

3 Cover the whole cupboard and doors with two coats of burgundy matt emulsion paint. Leave to dry. The 'stencil' used here was part of a soft, plastic tablecloth, probably from the fifties, which had a perforated lacy pattern on it. A piece of old lace fabric or paper doily would do as well. Mount your 'stencil' onto the outside of the glass door using spray adhesive. Stencil using white hard surface paint and the brush method (see page 108).

LEFT: *If necessary, the stencilled glass can be cleaned very gently, using cotton-wool wrapped sticks soaked in lighter fuel. Try not to wet the stencil paint. Alternatively, varnish with clear gloss polyurethane to create a wipe-clean surface.*

4 To achieve the crackle effect, dissolve 1 kilo (1 pound) of gum arabic crystals (from good art stores) in 1.5 litres (2–3 pints) of cold water heated up in an old saucepan until they become the consistency of single or light cream. Strain, if necessary, through a sieve and cool before use. Store in a jar with a lid.

5 Paint the gum arabic solution over the top, sides and handles of the cupboard. Leave overnight to dry, when the cracks will be clearly visible. With a wide brush, paint on the top coat of lime green matt emulsion. The entire area to be crackled must be done quickly, with no attempt made to overbrush any part already painted or the cracks will vanish before your eyes. Leave to dry and re-attach the doors.

ACCESSORIES

The home would be
a very barren place indeed without lots of ornaments
to provide interest and decoration. Anything from
lampshades to letter racks can be adorned with
stencilling to sit in pride of place in your own home, or
to be given as a unique gift to a special person.

THIRTIES FIRE SCREEN

DURING the summer when the fire is not lit, the fireplace can be a gaping hole in the wall. Filled with a decorative screen and fresh plants, it can be used as a focal point in the room. This 1930s screen was desperately in need of cheering up. Once painted and stencilled, it was transformed into a useful and striking accessory for the home.

RIGHT: *This firescreen needed to be painted because the original wood was of poor quality. The panel piece seemed to have been a packing case in a previous life! Pale shades were used to complement the whiteness of the marble fire surround and to pick out the colour scheme of the room.*

1 Some of the varnishes used in the thirties become very thick and sticky when coated with paint stripper – this was one of them! Wear protective rubber gloves and use lots of medium grade steel wool to remove it. The wool will become clogged very quickly so replace frequently and re-apply stripper if required. Allow to dry and sand down well (see page 102).

2 Paint the entire screen in off-white oil-based paint. If time is short, use an acrylic primer for an undercoat as this dries almost immediately. Oil-based and acrylic paints may be used indiscriminately together. When dry, cover the panel area with green oil-based paint. On a dark object such as this, you will need to apply at least three coats in total to cover.

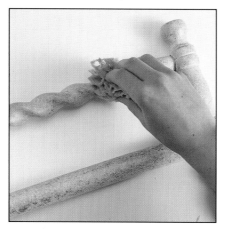

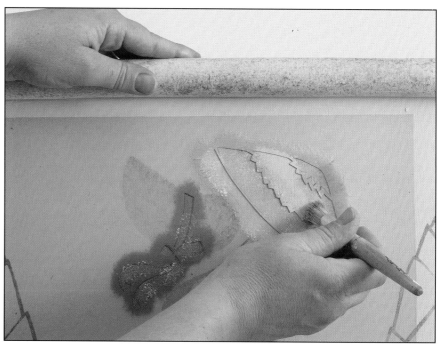

3 Add decorative touches reminiscent of the thirties. Sponging in gold was a favourite in those thrifty times as it made an object appear more luxurious than it really was. Use thinned acrylic gold paint, dabbing it on the edges only with a small natural sponge dampened in water. Use the templates on page 184 to cut stencils from plastic film for the Victorian lady, the flower, the tree and the crazy paving. Using the brush method (see page 108), stencil the lady in shades of pink, white, blue and cream hard-surface paints. Use brown, green and mauve paints to paint the remaining stencils. To stencil in reverse, clean the used side of the stencil with cellulose thinners in a well-ventilated room and turn over.

4 One of the beauties of stencilling is the facility of mixing colours on the stencil itself to give shading. This can create the impression of roundness, for example. On the lady's dress and umbrella, stencil white over pink on the left hand side as a highlight and add a darker pink on the other side to produce shadowing.

IVY-LEAF TIE-BACK

IF STENCILLING a whole curtain sounds a little daunting, try making tie-backs first. They are a quick and easy accessory to make from scraps of fabric left over from soft furnishing projects. Alternatively, make them in a toning colour, as shown here, or use a contrasting fabric for dramatic effect.

BELOW: If the brush is still wet after stencilling the tie-back fabric, continue the pattern along the wall to create a dado! A small repeating design like this breaks up a flat, coloured wall beautifully.

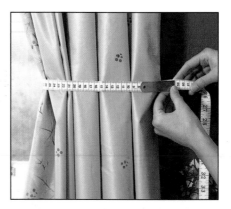

1 LEFT: Plain, ready-made curtains are ideal subjects for stencilling. Here, the main motif is stencilled on the inside border edge and the remaining area covered with a tiny pattern of berries. Use the template on page 182 to cut an ivy leaf stencil from plastic film (see page 106). Stencil with fabric paints in soft green, green, red, yellow, orange and white, using the brush method (see page 108). Keep the stencil in place on the fabric with spray adhesive. For the tie-back, measure around your curtain with a tape measure to find the length of fabric required. Add 3 cm (1⅛ in) hem allowance.

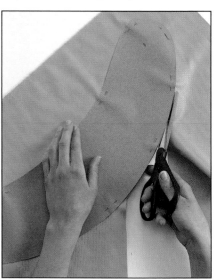

2 Halve the tie-back measurement. Draw onto folded paper the outline of a curved tie-back to this measurement. Cut out and open. Use this pattern to cut two pieces of fabric and a lining of heavy-weight stiffening. Use the template on page 182 to cut a stencil from the ivy leaf and berries motif (see page 106). Stencil onto the right side of the front tie-back piece, using red, yellow, orange and green fabric paints and referring to the brush stencilling method on page 108. Make a length of piping in a darker or contrasting colour and machine sew around the edges of the front piece on the right side (see page 111). Cover on the right side with the back piece and lining. Sew around the edge, leaving a gap for turning. Trim the raw edges and clip the curves, turn to the right side and sew the opening closed. Sew a metal ring to the wrong side of each end of each tie-back and attach tie-back hooks to the wall.

GINGHAM SHELF EDGING

Simple to make, shelf edging transforms plain cupboards and dressers in the kitchen, creating a sense of unity between shelves displaying a variety of items. The colour scheme used here may not suit you and you may prefer to pick a colour that either tones with that of the objects you are displaying or one that reflects the colour scheme used in the room you are decorating.

RIGHT: Position the shelf edging just below the top edge of the shelf so that a neat line of wood is visible. This adds to the overall decorative effect. Replace the fabric lining with another paper one, or even add a third layer if the distance between the shelves is very great.

BELOW: Make a double-layered edging, backing the stencilled paper with fabric. Here the geometric design of the wallpaper is matched with similarly patterned gingham.

1 Cut a 6 cm (2¼ in) deep strip of green paper to the length of your shelf. Divide the length by 5 cm (2 in) to determine the number of 'v's. Mark the uppermost point of each 'v' 1.5 cm (½ in) away from one edge, then mark the bottom-most points. Cut out with a sharp scalpel and steel rule. Using a one-hole punch, make a pattern of holes along the top edge, positioning the hole directly above the point through which to weave the ribbon and as decoration on each point. Cut a stencil (see page 106) from the bow template on page 182. Stencil in burgundy using hard-surface paint and a stencil brush (see page 108).

2 Choose a closely-woven green gingham fabric for the shelf edging lining; otherwise it will fray badly when cut. Press onto the reverse side of the fabric a length of light-weight iron-on interfacing as used in dressmaking. Cut as for the paper, marking the uppermost point of the 'v' 3 cm (1⅛ in) from the top edge of the fabric and the bottommost points 7.5 cm (3 in) away. Cut out carefully with pinking shears. Thread the holes along the top of the paper with three lengths of fine burgundy ribbon, one in the centre section and the others to either side. Secure with glue at the outer edges. Tie the loose ends in bows. Glue the gingham edging to the back of the paper with general purpose adhesive. Secure on the shelf with double-sided sticky tape.

HANDMADE GIFTWRAP

A BEAUTIFULLY wrapped present is a delight to receive, but one wrapped in hand-printed paper is quite wonderful! It is not difficult to stencil and make a gift box, or to give a plain book a stunning cover. Opening a hand-made card, too, shows much time and thought went into the greeting. Stencil tissue paper for packing, coloured card for postcards, even humble brown parcel paper can be subtly enhanced with gold stencilling.

BOOK JACKET

1 *Cut endpapers the size of the book cover and a piece of plain paper this size plus 2.5 cm (1 in). Using the templates on page 183, cut and paint the lily, thistle and daffodil motifs onto the endpapers and jacket. Centre the book over the wrong side of the paper and trim the corners, leaving 3 mm (⅛ in) of paper at the points. Make slits at the spine. Glue the wrong side of the jacket to the book. Close the book, sticking turnings to the inside. Glue on end papers. Trim excess paper off at the spine.*

GIFTWRAP

1 *Use dandelion leaves, ivy or flower heads to achieve 'reverse' stencilling. Lay them at random on paper. Thin acrylic paint slightly with water (gold and old copper were used here), dip the end of a stencil brush in it and flick the bristles with a forefinger to produce a fine spray. Remove the leaves or flower heads. Alternatively, stencil coloured or textured paper with a repeating pattern. Use the templates on page 183 to cut fritillaria and holly stencils (see page 106) and stencil with a brush (see page 108) in green, purple and red hard-surface paints.*

GIFT TAG

1 *Use the offcuts from making the gift box to stencil gift and name tags. To trim off the excess card around the stencilling cut straight lines, using a steel rule and a sharp craft knife or scalpel, but stop cutting where the stencilling overlaps. Trim around these overlaps by hand to give an interesting outline. In one corner, use a hole punch to make a hole to thread the ribbon through.*

ABOVE: *Purchase thin coloured card, which comes in a wonderful array of colours, from good stationers and art stores to make cards, gift boxes and tags. Make book jackets from heavy, good quality paper – it needs to be strong, hard-wearing, but pliable. Stencil your card with any of the motifs illustrated here to produce a personal and individual accompaniment to your gifts.*

GREETING CARDS

1 Cut window mount cards from thin coloured card to measure 33 x 15 cm (13 x 6 in). Fold in three, making folds as step 2 of the gift box. Cut a window from the centre section. Measure the width of your card aperture and add 1 cm (¼ in) to either side. Lay a steel rule on a piece of textured paper to this width and gently tear the paper towards you to produce a feathered edge. Tear again at right angles to form small pieces that fit the card appertures.

2 Use the cherub and fritillaria templates on page 183 to stencil the torn paper in gold, green and purple stencil paints with the brush method. Glue the stencilled paper to the wrong side of the first section. Glue around the wrong side of the window and fold over the first section, sticking it in place. Add decorative flourishes with coloured marker pens. Mark lines lightly in pencil around the aperture of the card, then draw over them, using the marker pen against a bevelled ruler face down on the card to prevent ink running under.

GIFT BOX

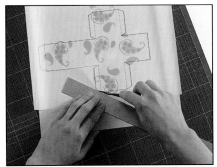 

1 Draw off the template for a gift box on page 183 onto tracing paper. Use this as a guide to the size of area that needs stencilling. Referring to the paisley group template on page 183, cut a stencil and paint a repeating paisley pattern onto a piece of thin, coloured card. Use the brush method and green, yellow, mauve and maroon stencil or acrylic paints. To cut out the box, lay the tracing over the card, tape in place with masking tape and cut out carefully along the solid lines only, using a sharp craft knife or scalpel on a cutting board.

2 Using the tracing as a guide, score lightly along the dotted lines with the knife on the stencilled side of the card. Bend carefully at the score lines until a right angle is formed in each case. Spread general purpose glue on the four tabs of the 'cross bar' and glue to the plain side of the 'upright' bar, forming a box. Fold down the lid, tucking in the tab to close.

QUILL AND PEN STATIONERY SET

L ETTER WRITING is still the most enduring form of communication, and all the more pleasurable if you have elegant accessories to use! Old letter racks, index files and blotters are easily found and can be renovated in subtle antique tones for the study, or in strong, eye-catching colours for the home office. Keep bills tidy, store family photographs or keep favourite magazine recipes in order with this attractive set of stationery items.

INDEX FILE

1 Remove the drawer from the box. Using a screwdriver with a fine head, carefully pull up the handle (this one was plastic) taking care not to damage the surface. Replace this with a brass handle or card carrier on completion.

2 This index file was made from a mixture of wood and thick cardboard. A wallpaper stripping agent will remove the paper from both if care is taken not to soak the cardboard too much. Once the liquid has soaked through the paper layer, gently prize it off with a metal scraper. Try to memorize the order of any overlaps or joins on the original paper.

3 Allow to dry thoroughly before covering with new paper. Select a good quality, plain one. Starting with the back of the box, cut the paper to fit, leaving 2 cm (¾ in) overlap all around. Paste the wrong side with PVA medium, press in place and trim the excess off the corners. Stick the overlapping paper to the sides. Cover the body of the box and the drawer in the same way and leave to dry. Use the templates on page 182 to cut a quill and pen motif and two small oak leaf stencils (see page 106). Stencil with a brush (see page 108) in red, green, navy, black and gold hard-surface paints. Mask off the oak leaf design around the pen and quill when stencilling these to prevent colours from accidentally mixing.

LETTER RACK

1 Remove the varnish finish from the wood (see page 102). It is at this point that the final finish must be decided on. Should the wood turn out to have beautiful graining, it would be a shame to paint it. Fill any holes or scratches with fine surface filler, using a metal filler knife. Sand smooth when dry (see page 102).

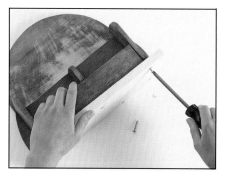

2 The base feet and the original thirties plastic feet on this letter rack were replaced. Where possible, use the original screw holes, drilling holes to match in the new base piece. Tiny wooden door handles were used as replacement feet. Stick in place with wood glue. Apply two coats of eggshell in two shades of blue. In a well-ventilated room, clean the stencils cut for the index file with cellulose thinners. Stencil the motifs onto the letter rack as described for the index file.

BLOTTER

1 Gilding is a wonderful method of creating instant age and makes a very ordinary object look expensive. Purchase red fontenay paste, gilt cream and optional gilt patina pencils from good art stores. Prepare the surface of an old blotter to reveal bare wood by stripping or sanding off old paint or varnish. Paint the handle and top of the blotter with fonteney paste. Allow to dry. Paint the curved underpart with two coats of blue eggshell. Leave to dry.

2 Paint over the red fontenay paste with gilt cream, using a stiffish brush. Dry, then sand off gently in places with fine grade steel wool to reveal the red layer beneath. With a clean cloth, buff to a soft sheen. The object can be left like this or more ageing and highlights added with patina pencils. Crayon them on in tiny lines or in small areas. Refer to step 3 of the index file to decorate the curved underpart of the blotter by stencilling with the small oak leaf motifs.

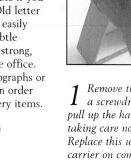

CANDLESTICKS

1 The original finish on these candlesticks was so fine they only needed a light rub with medium grade steel wool to give a 'key' for the paint. Wrap the steel wool around an area and rotate the candlestick within it, to create a smooth surface. Finish with fine grade wool and paint with two coats of blue eggshell. The metal areas were painted in copper, an artist's brush being dipped into a small amount of paint sprayed into the lid of the can. Clean brushes in turpentine.

2 To unify the metal and wood and create an up-to-the-minute look, try a verdigris effect on the metal. Verdigris is traditionally done in shades of green but use blue tones here. Follow the verdigris directions on page 104 to make up two blue pastes. Take care not to get it on the paintwork and wipe off immediately with a damp cloth if you do. Sand carefully with fine steel wool to reveal the copper paint. Position the small oak leaf stencils cut for the index file on areas large enough for decoration. Stencil as before.

ABOVE: *Adapt a space under the stairs or display stationery items in a corner to show them to their best advantage. They will look particularly attractive arranged on natural wood in dark, rich colours. The candlesticks can also be used as table centrepieces or to decorate a mantelpiece.*

LEFT: *An index file was used to list names and addresses chronologically, but now its uses are endless. Classify a compact disc collection, notes on the family tree or just store odds and ends in it!*

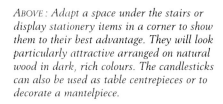

PICTURES AND FRAMES

IF EVERY PICTURE tells a story, then its stencilled frame tells another one! Old pictures and frames are so often designated to the scrap heap, but if you take a second look at them, they can become individual works of art with a little imagination. The easiest frames to stencil are wide and flat or with a gentle curve. But stencilling does not have to be confined to the frame – a large mount is ideal – or try stencilling the picture.

RIGHT: Old frames can be given a new lease of life with decorative stencilling while smaller pictures can be given additional impact by echoing the motif on the mount.

FRUIT FRAME

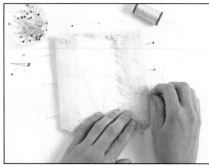

1 *Mount a piece of embroidery with a fruit motif by cutting a piece of white card to the outside measurements of the embroidered area, allowing a border all around. Place the card on the wrong side of the work and fold the excess fabric over the card. Secure by pushing pins into the edge of the card all around. Using a needle and buttonhole thread, secure the embroidery with stitches from top to bottom and from side to side. Oversew to secure and remove the pins. Ask a picture framing service to cut a mount to the measurements of your frame and with a circular aperture. Use the template on page 181 to cut a cherry stencil. With a brush and using gold hard-surface paint, stencil the cherries and three leaves only onto the corners of the mount, masking off the part of the stencil not needed. In red, orange, green and gold paints, stencil the whole motif onto the corners of the frame.*

LEFT: A large mount is very dramatic and leads the eye into the picture. Echo the subject matter subtly in gold stencilling and emphasize the frame edge, rubbing on acrylic gold paint with the tip of your finger.

SILHOUETTES FRAME

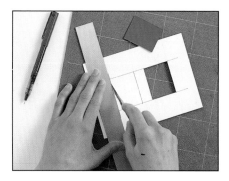

1 *For the mount, measure the recess of the frame and cut dark blue artist's card to this size using a sharp scalpel, a steel rule*

and a cutting board. On the wrong side mark two 4 x 5 cm (1½ x 2 in) apertures 1.5 cm (½ in) apart for the silhouettes with a fine marker pen. Cut these openings, finishing the cuts exactly on the marked lines. Cut a piece of white card to the same size as the mount. Lay the mount over the right side of the white card and lightly mark the openings in pencil. Use the templates on page 181 to cut and stencil two silhouettes onto the white card using black paint and a stencil brush (see pages 106 and 108). To verdigris a metal frame, follow the instructions given on pages 104–105. Replace the mount in the frame, followed by the stencilled silhouettes and backing board.

FLORAL FRAME

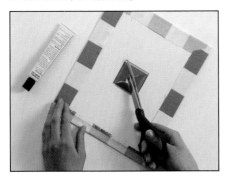

1 Take the backing board off the frame and prepare the wooden surface as described on page 102, including the final sanding. It is possible to lighten wood a little with a proprietary wood bleach. Wear rubber gloves and use a glass bowl. Dip a paintbrush in the liquid and paint on sparingly. Leave to dry and re-apply if necessary. Wash off and allow to dry. Cut three stencils from the rose and rosebud templates on page 181. Stencil the motifs onto the frame with a brush (see page 108), using two shades of green, and red, pink and white hard-surface paint. Cut a cardboard mount as for the silhouette frame, making a 5 cm (2 in) square aperture in the centre. Place the mount on large-checked blue fabric and cut 2.5 cm (1 in) larger all around. Trim away the fabric at each corner. Apply general purpose glue to the turnings and press to the wrong side of mount, keeping the fabric taut on the front. Snip into the corners of the central opening and glue the turnings to the mount in the same way.

2 Use the template on page 181 to cut a floral bouquet stencil. Stencil using the brush method in red, yellow and green paints onto the centre of a piece of white card. Cut to the same size as the mount. Fit the fabric mount then the stencilled picture into the frame. Replace the backing board. Moisten the gummed side of 5 cm (2 in) tape with a damp sponge and glue onto the back where the backing board and frame meet. Push the backing board down firmly. Screw in screw eyes with rings on either side of the frame and attach picture wire.

MIRROR

1 Remove the glass from a circular mirror frame approximately 30 cm (12 in) in diameter. Paint using acrylic paint in a copper tone. Replace the mirror. On white cartridge paper and using the oak leaf templates on page 181 to cut stencils, stencil 18 leaves with a stencil brush and acrylic paints in metallic shades of gold, bronze, red and copper. Using small, sharp scissors, cut around each leaf. Use diluted PVA medium to stick in place, overlapping one another and breaking onto the mirror surface. Clean off any glue with a damp cloth.

GOOSE FRAME

1 This charming embroidery was very badly marked as water, coloured by the wood mount, had stained the fabric. Remove the worst areas of discolouration and any spots with well-diluted household bleach applied gently on a cotton wool-wrapped stick (try a test area first). Lay the embroidery on kitchen paper towel while working. Replace the sticks frequently. Before remounting the embroidery, soak it in a solution of biological washing powder. Lay on kitchen paper towel to dry. Press.

2 Cut a piece of mounting board with an adhesive surface on one side, available from craft stores, to fit the embroidery. Peel off the paper covering and carefully lay the wrong side of the embroidery over the sticky area, starting from one corner and smoothing out any creases. Use the template on page 181 to cut and paint the geese stencils in white paint with a brush on the board. If necessary, have glass cut by a glazier to fit the frame. When re-assembling the picture, place the glass into the frame first. The gold fillet (the narrow edging on the inside of a frame) on this frame was in good enough condition and could be re-used.

2 From a 10 cm (4 in) wide strip of cotton fabric cut two pieces 35 cm (14 in) long for tails, one 60 cm (23½ in) length for loops and one 18 cm (7 in) length for a tie. Lay on a surface that can be cleaned. Paint each one on the wrong side with PVA adhesive and fold in the side edges to meet in the centre. Open out a carrier bag and on it place the ends of the loop together. Nip the centre of the circle with the 'tie' and insert the 'tails' under the tie. Support the loops with screwed up plastic bags and leave to dry. Paint with bronze acrylic paint.

ABOVE: Pick out details like flat edges in matching paint. The colour scheme is obviously red and blue. Both are present in the braid, which not only adds a finishing, decorative touch but unites the two colours.

FARMHOUSE KITCHENWARE

OLD FASHIONED enamelware is making a comeback in the kitchen. Copies of 1950s designs can be bought again, while original pieces can be found at flea markets and second-hand stores. These are often dented or chipped and are not to be recommended for use in the preparation of food. However, they are wonderful stencilled as decorative pieces out on display. Match them up with other items to give total co-ordination.

SCALES

1 The weighing bowl on this basic set of scales was made from tin. Much better looking are brass or copper bowls. Cheat a little and colour the bowl with brass, copper or bronze spray paint in a can. This bowl was painted brass to match the lovely brass weights that were bought with it. Two iron weights that were also part of the set were given several coats of blackboard paint before being stencilled to match the scales.

HERB DRAWERS

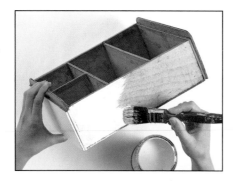

1 Create a set of herb drawers from an old miniature chest. This one, though crudely made from cheap timber, had good proportions and lovely china handles. These were carefully unscrewed and the old paint cleaned off with fine steel wool and paint stripper. Use rubber gloves if you can, or coat your hands with barrier cream to protect them. Strip off the old finish and sand smooth (see page 102). The entire surface need not be painted as a little natural wood showing adds to the country feel. Cover the areas to be painted with acrylic primer, masking the edges if necessary. Acrylic primer dries quickly, making handling easier when the whole object is not being painted. Cover the primed areas with pale green eggshell paint. Allow to dry. Remove masking tape.

2 Paint the base of the scales with red oxide metal primer (an awkward shape like these scales may need two coats to cover all the nooks and crannies). Then coat in a rich cream oil-based paint such as eggshell. Painting such a pale colour over the dark metal primer will require several coats. Dry well between coats.

RIGHT: Once no longer in use, old coffee and teapots make ideal objects for decorating with stencils and displaying in a kitchen cabinet, or on a dresser.

RIGHT: Old kitchenware often has particularly appealing shapes. You will probably have some old kitchenware yourself in your attic or storeroom.

BELOW: Pick items with varying shapes and heights to make an interesting display of kitchenware. These charming pieces, gathered from a variety of sources, are painted in clotted cream and herb shades and decorated with appropriate country images to fit the style and atmosphere of the kitchen decorated in farmhouse style.

TEAPOT AND COFFEEPOT

1 Even badly stained enamel, as often found in old teapots, can be cleaned effectively. Soak in a bowl of cold water and biological washing powder. Leave for a couple of days if necessary and scrub intermittantly with a pan scourer which will not scratch the surface.

2 Fill any chips or dents with two-part car filler, available from car accessory stores, following the manufacturer's directions for use. Any rust should be treated with a rust removal product. Paint the object inside and out with red oxide metal primer. In damp weather, the inside may take several days to dry. Paint on several coats of green or cream eggshell paint. Allow each coat to dry thoroughly before painting the next.

STENCILLING

1 Use the templates on page 185 to cut stencils of the floral and cow motifs (see page 106). Stencil onto the tea and coffee pot base and lid, the base of the scales and iron weights and onto the front of each herb drawer. Stencil with a brush (see page 108) in soft shades of green, pink, blue and brown hard-surface paints. Use spray adhesive and masking tape to keep the stencils in place. Pick out any details on the pots using one of the stencilling colours and an artist's paint brush to colour knobs and rims. To age your kitchenware, try crackling it, using one of the varieties of crackling varnish available from good paint and art stores. Follow the manufacturer's directions carefully.

2 When the crackling is quite dry, make up an ageing solution to patinate or darken the cracks. Mix some artist's oil paint in a burnt umber shade with a little turpentine to the consistency of double or heavy cream. Paint it all over – do not worry if it looks like a dreadful mistake. Allow to dry for a few minutes before wiping off the excess with a clean rag. Leave the paint in the cracks to dry. The entire surface of your kitchenware will be slightly darkend by using this treatment. Paint with polyurethane varnish if desired.

Diagrams and Stencils

The following pages present the templates for the stencils used in this book. To reproduce the templates at the same size as originally used for each project, either trace the motif straight from the page where the motif is designated 'same size', or enlarge the motif to the percentage given on a photocopier. Otherwise, use a photocopier to enlarge or reduce the motif to the size required for your model.

A number of motifs will require you to cut two or more separate stencils where one colour is stencilled over another (see pages 106–107). The number of stencils to be cut is specified in each case.

ROSE CHEST OF DRAWERS
page 114

BOW
Enlarge by 150%
Cut 1

SMALL ROSE
Same size
Cut 1

LARGE ROSE
Enlarge by 150%
Cut 1

ORIENTAL WARDROBE
page 116

DRAGONFLY 1
Enlarge by 200%
Cut 1

DRAGONFLY 2
Enlarge by 200%
Cut 1

Place to fold

CHINESE CIRCLE
Enlarge by 200%
Cut 1

BIRD
Enlarge by 200%
Cut 1

TREE SECTION (LEFT)
Enlarge by 200%
Cut 1

169

FLORAL CIRCULAR TABLE
page 118

OUTER MOTIF
Enlarge by 150%
Cut 3

CENTRAL MOTIF
Enlarge by 150%
Cut 1

TARTAN DINING CHAIRS
page 120

TARTAN
Enlarge by 200%
Cut 3

HEART CUPBOARD
page 122

HEART & RIBBON
Same size
Cut 1

GRID
Enlarge by 150%
Cut 1

FLOWER
Enlarge by 150%
Cut 1

ART NOUVEAU FIREPLACE
page 124

MOTIF
Enlarge by 150%
Cut 1

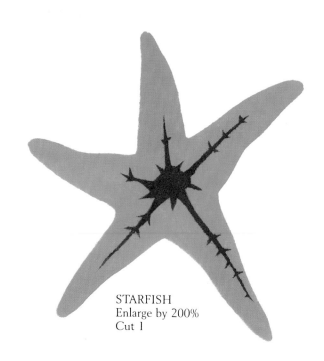

SHELL
Enlarge by 200%
Cut 1

SHELL
Enlarge by 200%
Cut 1

STARFISH
Enlarge by 200%
Cut 1

NOAH'S ARK COT QUILT
page 130

LION
Enlarge by 150%
Cut 3

ARK
Enlarge by150%
Cut 1

ELEPHANTS
Enlarge by 150%
Cut 1

SQUIRREL
Enlarge by150%
Cut 2

GIRAFFE
Enlarge by 150%
Cut 2

NOAH'S WIFE
Enlarge by 150%
Cut 2

NOAH
Enlarge by150%
Cut 2

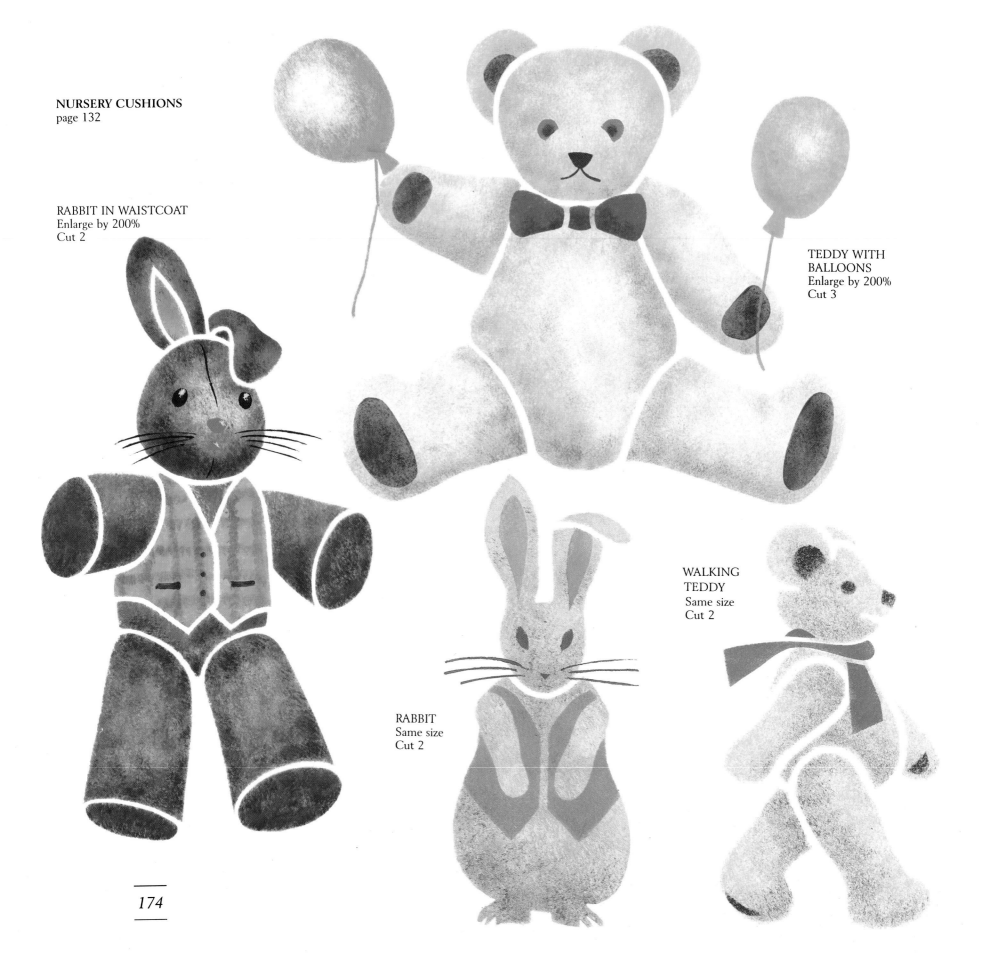

NURSERY CUSHIONS
page 132

RABBIT IN WAISTCOAT
Enlarge by 200%
Cut 2

TEDDY WITH
BALLOONS
Enlarge by 200%
Cut 3

WALKING
TEDDY
Same size
Cut 2

RABBIT
Same size
Cut 2

EGYPTIAN BATHROOM
page 134

FLOWER
Same size
Cut 1

PALM TREE
Same size
Cut 1

FLOWER
Same size
Cut 1

WATER CARRIER
Same size
Cut 1

SPHINX
Same size
Cut 1

CLASSIC RUG
page 136

CLASSIC MOTIF 1
Same size
Cut 1

CLASSIC MOTIF 2
Same size
Cut 1

176

SEA CREATURES DECKCHAIR
page 138

FISH
Same size
Cut 1

SEA MONSTER
Enlarge by 150%
Cut 1

SEA MONSTER
Same size
Cut 1

177

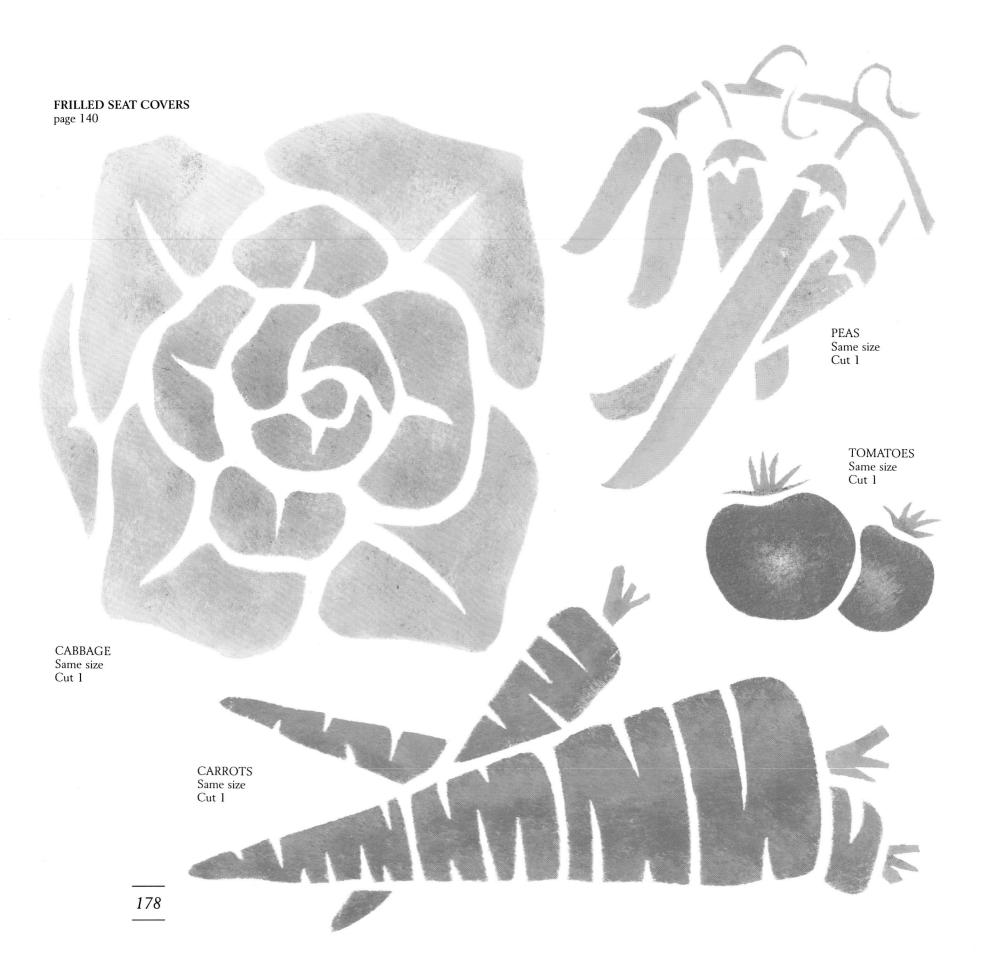

FRILLED SEAT COVERS
page 140

PEAS
Same size
Cut 1

TOMATOES
Same size
Cut 1

CABBAGE
Same size
Cut 1

CARROTS
Same size
Cut 1

FRENCH BREAD BIN
page 146

TREES, HEDGE, GATE
Enlarge by 150%
Cut 1

CHIVES
Enlarge by 150%
Cut 2

MOUSE
Same size
Cut 2

CAT
Enlarge by 200%
Cut 2

CHILD'S DRESSER
page 148

BOOKS
Enlarge by 150%
Cut 1

STANDING DOLL
Enlarge by 150%
Cut 2

SITTING DOLL
Enlarge by 150%
Cut 2

PLATE
Enlarge by 150%
Cut 1

CUP AND SAUCER
Enlarge by 150%
Cut 1

TEDDY
Enlarge by 150%
Cut 1

PICTURES AND FRAMES
page 164

SILHOUETTE 1
Same size
Cut 1

SILHOUETTE 2
Same size
Cut 1

FLORAL BOUQUET
Same size
Cut 1

ROSE
Same size
Cut 1

ROSEBUDS
Same size
Cut 1 each

GEESE
Same size
Cut 1

OAK LEAVES
Same size
Cut 1

CHERRIES
Same size
Cut 1

181

FROSTED DOOR PANELS
page 150

IVY LEAF TIE-BACK
page 158

ART NOUVEAU MOTIF
Enlarge by 200%
Cut 1

IVY LEAF
Enlarge by 200%
Cut 2

GINGHAM SHELF EDGING
page 159

LEAF AND BERRIES
Enlarge by 150%
Cut 1

BOW
Same size
Cut 1

**QUILL AND PEN
STATIONERY SET**
page 162

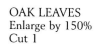

QUILL AND PEN
Enlarge by 150%
Cut 1

OAK LEAVES
Enlarge by 150%
Cut 1

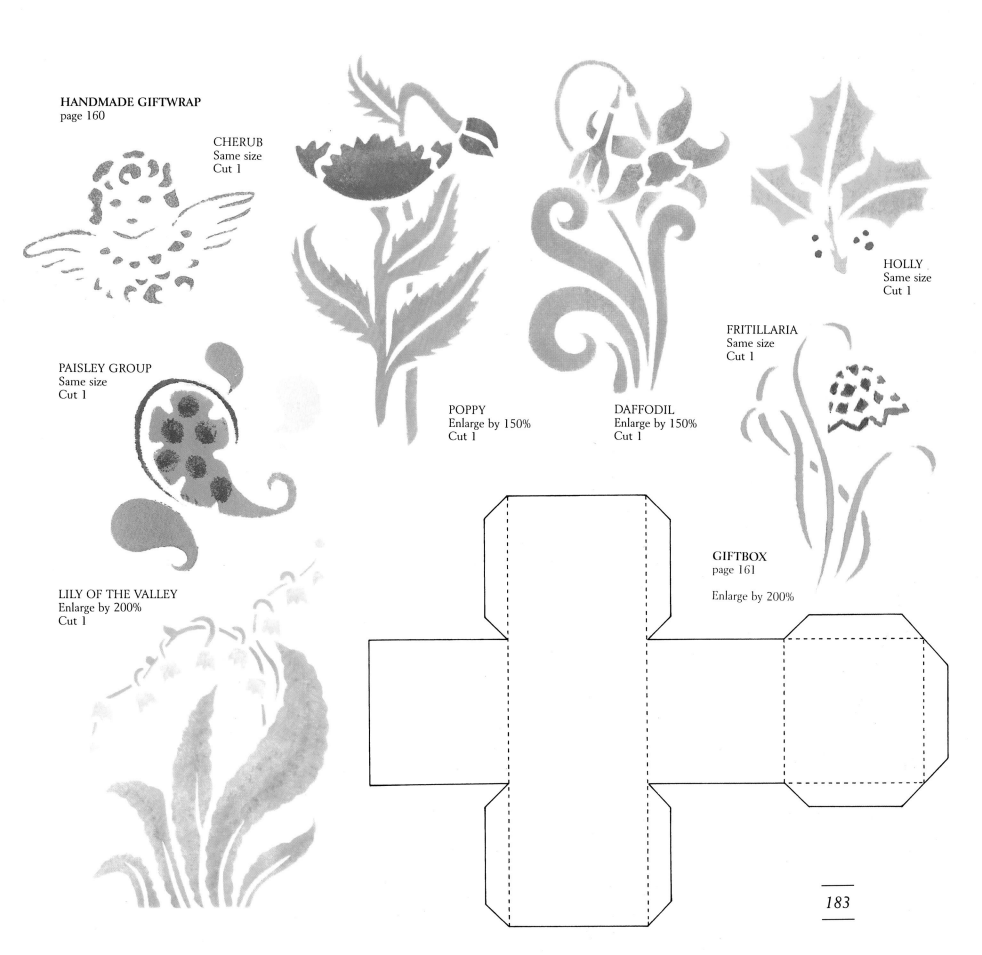

HANDMADE GIFTWRAP
page 160

CHERUB
Same size
Cut 1

HOLLY
Same size
Cut 1

FRITILLARIA
Same size
Cut 1

PAISLEY GROUP
Same size
Cut 1

POPPY
Enlarge by 150%
Cut 1

DAFFODIL
Enlarge by 150%
Cut 1

GIFTBOX
page 161

Enlarge by 200%

LILY OF THE VALLEY
Enlarge by 200%
Cut 1

VICTORIAN FIRESCREEN
page 156

VICTORIAN LADY
Enlarge by 200%
Cut 2

TREE
Enlarge by 200%
Cut 1

FLOWER
Enlarge by 200%
Cut 1

CRAZY PAVING
Enlarge by 200%
Cut 1

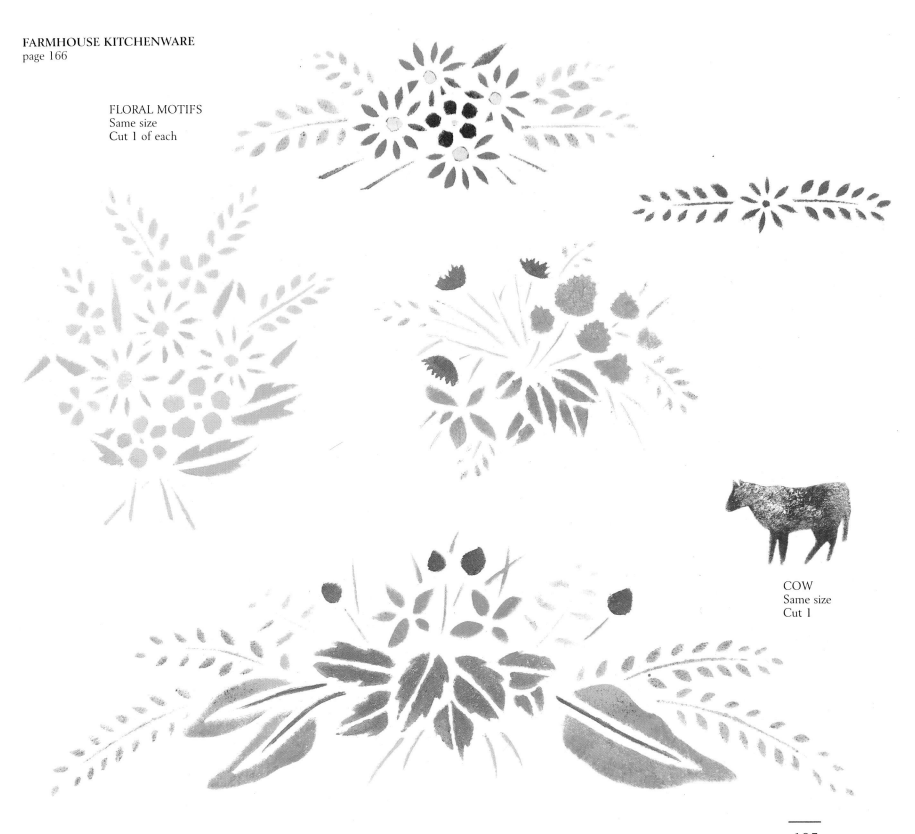

FARMHOUSE KITCHENWARE
page 166

FLORAL MOTIFS
Same size
Cut 1 of each

COW
Same size
Cut 1

GEOMETRIC PATIO & POTS
page 144

POT BORDER 1
Enlarge by 150%
Cut 1

POT STAR
Enlarge by 150%
Cut 1

POT BORDER 2
Enlarge by 150%
Cut 1

MOSAIC BORDER
Enlarge by 150%
Cut 1

MOSAIC CORNER
Enlarge by 150%
Cut 1

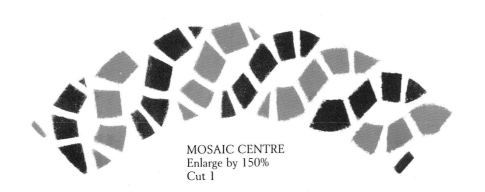

MOSAIC CENTRE
Enlarge by 150%
Cut 1

**HERE IS A SELECTION OF UNUSUAL STENCILS
WHICH CAN BE USED AROUND THE HOME**

BORDER LEAVES

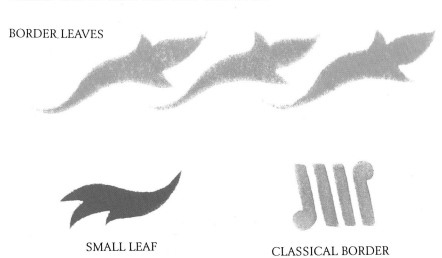

SMALL LEAF

CLASSICAL BORDER

FLEUR-DE-LYS

ROSE BOUQUET

HALF STAR

Glossary

Some of the terms used in this book may be found under a different name:

Glasspaper: use coarse sandpaper
Fine grade flour paper: use finest sandpaper
Methylated spirit: use denatured alcohol
Scumble glaze: simply use either stipple glaze or simple glaze
Sugar soap: use industrial strength non foaming detergent